MOSES

VOL. IV

MOSES' GREATEST MOMENTS

by Theodore H. Epp
Director
Back to the Bible Broadcast

A
BACK TO THE BIBLE
PUBLICATION

Back to the Bible
Lincoln, Nebraska 68501

85,000 printed to date—1976
(5-5017—85M—56)
ISBN 0-8474-1238-5

Printed in the United States of America

Contents

Chapter 1

The Broken Law

After Moses was used of God to lead the children of Israel out of Egypt, they came to Mount Sinai. There they were to receive the great revelation of God, commonly known as the "Law" or the "Mosaic Law."

The Israelites gathered at the foot of Mount Sinai, although they were instructed by God not to touch the mountain, or they would die (Ex. 19:12,13). The Lord called Moses to the top of Mount Sinai and then instructed him to return to the people and warn them again not to touch the mountain (vv. 20-24).

God then spoke what are commonly referred to as the "Ten Commandments" (20:1-17). "All the people saw the thunderings, and the lightnings, and the noise of the trumpet, and the mountain smoking: and when the people saw it, they removed, and stood afar off. And they said unto Moses, Speak thou with us, and we will hear: but let not God speak with us, lest we die" (vv. 18,19). The people were filled with awe and fear at this mighty revelation of God.

Three Aspects of Giving the Law

There were three aspects to the giving of the Law. First, there was the oral giving of the Law when God Himself spoke directly to the people as they stood at the foot of the mountain (Ex. 20:1-17). God had a very important purpose for speaking directly to the people. No such direct communication was made concerning laws of the priesthood or the various sacrifices; only the Ten Commandments were given in this way. Such an unusual communication, as well as the phenomena that accompanied it, let the people know for sure that the message was of God. It also clearly established Moses in their eyes as God's mediator between them and Him. No one had ever seen such an awesome display; there was no mistaking that God was giving Moses the Law.

A second aspect of the giving of the Law involved Moses' being called to the mountaintop to receive the tables of stone, which were engraved by God Himself (24:12-18). These contained the Ten Commandments, and it was these tables of stone that Moses broke when he came down from the mountain and discovered the people worshiping an idol.

The third aspect of the giving of the Law included the producing of a second set of stone tables after the first had been broken (34:1,28,29). These, too, were engraved by God Himself.

In connection with the oral giving of the Law, God also gave Moses some regulations and judgments concerning personal relationships—Hebrew to Hebrew. God did not give only ten commandments; many others were included in the Law. Later, the ceremonial law associated with the tabernacle was given on the mountaintop.

A Warning and a Covenant

Following God's oral communication of the Ten Commandments to Israel, He warned the people not to make any gods of silver or gold. Within the Ten Commandments God had specifically said, "Thou shalt not make unto thee any graven image, or any likeness of any thing that is in heaven above, or that is in the earth beneath, or that is in the water under the earth" (20:4). Then after the people responded in fear and trembling, God again said, "Ye shall not make with me gods of silver, neither shall ye make unto you gods of gold" (v. 23). From this time on others were told not to make gods of silver and gold, but only Israel had the specific privilege of hearing God orally communicate this prohibition. More than anyone else, Israel had conclusive proof that this command was directly from God.

Before Moses went up on the mountaintop to spend 40 days and 40 nights there, he communicated to the people the words and judgments of the Lord. The people responded by saying, "All the words which the Lord hath said will we do" (24:3). The people were quick to obligate themselves to the commands of God, and they even repeated their willingness to do anything the Lord said: "All that the Lord hath said will we do, and be obedient" (v. 7).

This covenant, or agreement, was ratified by blood from offerings: "Moses took the blood, and sprinkled it on the people, and said, Behold the blood of the covenant, which the Lord hath made with you concerning all these words" (v. 8).

Moses on the Mountain

After Moses had done this, the Lord told him, "Come up to me into the mount, and be there: and I will give thee tables of stone, and a law, and commandments which I have written; that thou mayest teach them" (24:12).

Joshua, who is well known because of the book which bears his name, went partway up the mountain with Moses: "Moses rose up, and his minister Joshua: and Moses went up into the mount of God" (v. 13). As Moses left the people, he delegated the authority to take care of any problems that arose while he was away to Aaron and Hur (v. 14).

While on the mountaintop, Moses waited for six days while a cloud covered the mountain. Then on the seventh day God "called unto Moses out of the midst of the cloud" (v. 16). As Moses later recorded this incident, he wrote: "The sight of the glory of the Lord was like devouring fire on the top of the mount in the eyes of the children of Israel" (v. 17). What a display of the glory of God! Israel was given the opportunity to observe the awesome sight of the presence of God as He revealed Himself to Moses. Moses was on the mountaintop communicating with God for 40 days and nights (v. 18).

Exodus 25—31 records the various instructions and regulations God gave to Moses concerning the tabernacle. God then interrupted His communication with Moses to tell him of the hideous sin the Israelites were committing at the foot of the mountain. Exodus 32—34 tells of this awful sin, but these chapters also reveal in depth the character of Moses. They reveal his holy anger against sin, his firmness in

judging sin and his greatest moments of love and intercession
for the people of Israel. That time of intercession in behalf of
his people was possibly the finest moment of Moses' life.
These three chapters of Exodus (32—34) center around
Israel's great sin as Aaron led them in worshiping false gods
while Moses was on the mountaintop with God.

What a contrast the Book of Exodus presents! On the one
hand we read of God's grace as He revealed to Moses His plan
of love, grace and mercy toward Israel (chs. 25—31). On the
other hand we read of that which exhibits the awful
depravity of fallen man—the worship of false gods (ch. 32).
On the one hand we see unveiled the manifold glories of
Christ, but on the other hand we see exposed the awful
abominations which Satan produces. On the one hand God
revealed for His people the provision for godly worship; on
the other hand we see the Israelites bowing down to worship
the idolatrous golden calf.

The majestic awesomeness of God's presence was made
known to the people. In fact, they could see it even while
they were sinning. They feared God only until He was a little
farther away.

At first He came down to the people. Then He moved to
the mountaintop where He and Moses could be alone. When
the people were left alone with Aaron as their leader, they
revealed the true attitude of their hearts. This attitude had
come to the surface numerous times before as they traveled
from Egypt to Sinai, but in the absence of Moses, they threw
away all restraint. Having convinced themselves that
something had happened to their chosen leader, the people
turned for leadership to something that had just been
expressly forbidden by God—false gods.

After the Lord had communicated with Moses, He gave
him "two tables of testimony, tables of stone, written with
the finger of God" (31:18). But at the foot of the mountain
the people gave up hope of Moses' ever returning because he
had been gone from them for 40 days and 40 nights. In
seeking for leadership, they told Aaron, "Up, make us gods,
which shall go before us; for as for this Moses, the man that
brought us up out the land of Egypt, we wot [know] not
what is become of him" (32:1).

Forgetfulness and Impatience

The New Testament Book of the Acts refers to Israel's attitude at this point. When Stephen defended his preaching after the resurrection of Christ, he reminded the Jewish leaders, "In their hearts [they] turned back again into Egypt, saying unto Aaron, Make us gods to go before us: for as for this Moses, which brought us out of the land of Egypt, we wot not what is become of him" (7:39,40). This is the key—within their hearts they turned back to Egypt.

The people of Israel were not angry with Moses because he lingered on the mountaintop for 40 days. Rather, they were impatient and were quick to forget God's dealings with them. It had only been three months since they had come out of Egypt. They had experienced the miracle of the Passover, in which God spared the firstborn of the Israelites and destroyed those of the Egyptians, and they had experienced the miracle at the Red Sea, which allowed the Israelites to pass through on dry ground whereas the pursuing Egyptians were drowned. Then God had provided water, manna and meat for them by His miracle-working power. Yet they were quick to forget all that God had done for them. At Mount Sinai, while Moses was actually receiving the Law, they cast off their allegiance to Jehovah, the ever-present One.

But even while the Israelites were doing this, God knew all that was going on. When God had spoken to the people, it had terrified them. Then the cloud enveloped the mountaintop for six days before God began communing alone with Moses. God had not moved away from them; He had only moved to the mountaintop, and the cloud was within their sight.

Moses had been on the mountaintop 40 days and nights, or about six weeks. Although the people couldn't see God or Moses, who was with Him, the cloud was still a visible evidence of His presence. But the people grew cynical and impatient, and then their hearts turned to false gods.

How easily we forget when God has spoken to us. Maybe He has spoken to us through an accident in the family or among our close acquaintances. Perhaps there has been a death, and we have been awed at such a tragedy. But soon it is forgotten again, and our hearts are no longer tender toward God. It's possible that God allowed whatever took place to happen so that He could get our attention and cause us to see our spiritual need. But how quickly the human heart turns from God, and we refuse to let Him deal with our soul's need.

The Israelites somehow forgot that God had been leading them so gloriously and wonderfully during the three months since they had come out of Egypt. Nevertheless, they did not forget the idols of Egypt. Even much later Joshua had to remind them to put away the gods which their fathers had served in Egypt (Josh. 24:14).

From the Israelites we see what a terrible thing the fretfulness of impatience is. From the time they left Egypt they had shown their impatience. They were impatient at the Red Sea when they were hemmed in. At the waters of Marah and at Rephidim when they needed water to drink, they were impatient not only with their leader, Moses, but also with God Himself. They did not realize that God was using these exact circumstances to teach them patience.

How much the Israelites were like believers today! It is so easy to forget all that God has done for us in the past, and we fail so often to see that He is trying to teach us valuable lessons as we pass through trials. Someone has described impatience as an attempt to do for oneself what God has not done or has delayed to do. As such, impatience is the enemy of faith.

The Results of Impatience

Abraham is a good illustration of one who became impatient with the promises of God and could no longer wait for God to act. Genesis 16 tells the sad story. Abraham could no longer wait for God to fulfill His promise to provide a son. As a result of his impatience, Ishmael was born to Abraham and Hagar, but Abraham was later to experience great anxiety because of this lack of patience.

At Mount Sinai, Israel's impatience resulted in idolatry. They refused to wait on the Lord. And even today, waiting on the Lord is a lost art. Believers today don't seem to have time to wait on the Lord. They rush here and there, involved in all kinds of activities, but don't give enough attention to getting the direction of the Lord before they rush off. Waiting does not mean sitting in a rocking chair, twiddling your thumbs, expecting God to do something sensational; rather, waiting on the Lord is simply putting your confidence in Him and waiting for God to act at His chosen time.

God didn't really need 40 days to reveal to Moses all that He had or to produce the two tables of stone with the Law on them. This length of time that Moses was on the mountaintop was just another test for the people of Israel. They were quick to say that they would obey the Lord (Ex. 24:3,7), but when Moses was gone from them for only six weeks, they turned to false gods.

Faith must be tried, not to prove to God that it is genuine, because He knows what is in the heart, but to show the person involved whether or not he has genuine faith. The New Testament says, "That the trial of your faith, being much more precious than of gold that perisheth, though it be tried with fire, might be found unto praise and honour and glory at the appearing of Jesus Christ" (I Pet. 1:7).

Much time had gone into God's dealing with Moses so God could show him the true character of his faith. It took 80 years of patient training for Moses to be what God wanted him to be.

Aaron Makes an Image

Because of impatience the Israelites called on Aaron to make them some gods to follow, since they did not know what had happened to Moses. This would have been an opportune time for Aaron to have taken a strong position and to have admonished the Israelites for their lack of faith and patience. But instead, notice what Aaron told them: "Break off the golden earrings, which are in the ears of your wives, of your sons, and of your daughters, and bring them unto me" (Ex. 32:2). Perhaps Aaron chose this particular means because he knew what they requested was wrong, and he wanted to make it hard for them. Perhaps he thought they would change their minds if they realized what it would cost them. But regardless of what he thought, they did not change their minds. "All the people brake off the golden earrings

which were in their ears, and brought them unto Aaron"
(v. 3).

Aaron still did not rebuke them for turning away from
God; instead, "he received them at their hand, and fashioned
it with a graving tool, after he had made it a molten calf: and
they said, These be thy gods, O Israel, which brought thee up
out of the land of Egypt" (v. 4).

It is incredible to think that Aaron would do something
like this after he had been so closely related to Moses in his
dealings with God. But notice what else Aaron did: "When
Aaron saw it, he built an altar before it; and Aaron made
proclamation, and said, To morrow is a feast to the Lord"
(v. 5).

Aaron and Hur had been left to look after the affairs of
Israel while Moses was absent. Joshua, Moses' servant, had
gone partway up the mountain with Moses, so he was not
with the people at the time of this sin. But while Moses was
on the mountaintop speaking to God face to face, the people
wanted some likeness to worship as a substitute. The people
were never allowed to see God face to face, but they knew
He was on the mountaintop because of all the evidences they
saw. But they wanted something they could feel with their
hands, something they could see.

The religion of the natural man demands something he
can perceive with his eyes. That is why so many people
today—even Christians—go after things that are earthly. They
need the security that is provided only by what they are able
to touch and see.

The Israelites were no different; they wanted a god they
could see. Moses was gone, and because their eyes had been
on him rather than on God, they wanted an image. Perhaps
this is why God took Moses away from them for a time. God
not only wanted to talk to Moses face to face, but He also
wanted to reveal to the Israelites that they were not really
trusting God as they thought they were. What a lesson this is
for believers today! Our trust should be in God, not in man.

A Prophet and a Priest

In order for us to better understand the situation Aaron
faced, it is necessary to examine more closely the difference

between the ministries of Moses and Aaron. Moses was a prophet; Aaron was a priest. There is a vast difference in these two offices. A prophet went before God to receive a divine message and then went before the people to speak on behalf of God. Thus, he represented God before man.

In one sense, preachers today are prophets since they deliver the message from God's Word to the people, but they are not prophets in the technical sense such as Moses was.

Moses was on the mountaintop receiving new revelation from God, but the people at the foot of the mountain were impatient. They just could not wait any longer for God's word. We frequently act in the same way; we do not take time to study the Word of God as we should. This is why the Word of God never seems to affect the lives of many believers even though they hear fine messages.

Moses was a prophet, but Aaron was a priest. The roles of a prophet and a priest were completely opposite. A prophet represented a holy God before sinful man; a priest represented sinful man before a holy God.

A prophet and a priest were equally important even though they had distinctively different functions. Another contrast of the two ministries is that a prophet declared doctrine—he gave God's teaching to the people. On the other hand, a priest declared experience—he presented the experiences of people to God. Doctrine and experience are related, but experience must come out of doctrine. Doctrine must not come out of experience.

Some people have an experience and then go to the Scriptures in an attempt to substantiate what they have experienced. They are really trying to build a doctrine on the basis of experience rather than making sure their experience is based on proper doctrine. We face many problems in evangelicalism today that are related to this matter of wanting to determine doctrine by experience. The believer should always move from doctrine to experience, never from experience to doctrine.

Christ as Prophet, Priest and King

Three great offices known in the Old Testament were prophet, priest and king. The Lord Jesus Christ is qualified to fill each of these positions. When He came to earth, He filled the position of prophet, for He declared God's message of love, grace and mercy to mankind. Having shed His blood for the forgiveness of sins and having ascended to heaven, Christ is now the priest of all those who call on Him. He represents their needs to the Heavenly Father. The Apostle John reminded his readers of this when he said, "My little children, these things write I unto you, that ye sin not. And if any man sin, we have an advocate with the Father, Jesus Christ the righteous" (I John 2:1). The Lord Jesus Christ is at the Father's side interceding in behalf of believers.

Referring to the Lord Jesus Christ, Hebrews 7:25 says, "Wherefore he is able also to save them to the uttermost that come unto God by him, seeing he ever liveth to make intercession for them." He is able to intercede for believers because He understands their needs. "Seeing then that we have a great high priest, that is passed into the heavens, Jesus the Son of God, let us hold fast our profession. For we have not an high priest which cannot be touched with the feeling of our infirmities; but was in all points tempted like as we are, yet without sin. Let us therefore come boldly unto the throne of grace, that we may obtain mercy, and find grace to help in time of need" (4:14-16).

Someday, Jesus Christ will return as king. The Bible refers to Him as "King of Kings, and Lord of Lords" (Rev. 19:16). The Lord Jesus Christ will rule personally on earth during the thousand-year kingdom (20:1-6).

Aaron's Weak Leadership

It was normal for the Israelites to approach Aaron with their request, because he was their priest to represent them before God. They thought Moses would never return, and they wanted divine guidance for the future, so they came to Aaron with their proposal.

But how could Aaron, who had witnessed and had assisted in the performance of the miracles in Egypt, be so forgetful and so blind that he yielded to Israel's whims and wishes? Aaron had personally seen that the gods of Egypt had no power, yet when he was asked to produce a god, he went along with the request. Without question, Aaron knew that God's presence was on the mountain with Moses, yet knowing this, he still gave in to the wishes of the Israelites.

God calls for and needs true and fearless leadership. Moses had been prepared by God for a period of 80 years, but Aaron had only one year of preparation in Egypt. Aaron was a weak leader from the beginning. The perils of weak leadership are exemplified in Aaron.

In the first crisis he faced after having been put in the position of responsibility, Aaron totally failed. He became a compromiser, a situation adapter, a servant of the people. His weakness was also seen later in the excuses he gave to Moses and in his outright lying about the golden calf. He sought only to justify himself.

While God was communicating with Moses on the mountaintop, He confronted Moses with what was taking place below. He said to Moses, "Go, get thee down; for thy people, which thou broughtest out of the land of Egypt, have corrupted themselves: they have turned aside quickly out of the way which I commanded them: they have made them a molten calf, and have worshipped it, and have sacrificed thereunto, and said, These be thy gods, O Israel, which have brought thee up out of the land of Egypt" (Ex. 32:7,8).

Earlier, when God spoke before all the people, He had specifically told them: "Thou shalt not make unto thee any graven image, or any likeness of any thing that is in heaven above, or that is in the earth beneath, or that is in the waters under the earth. Thou shalt not bow down thyself to them, nor serve them: for I the Lord thy God am a jealous God, visiting the iniquity of the fathers upon the children unto the third and fourth generation of them that hate me" (20:4,5).

To what God had spoken, the people had answered, "All the words which the Lord hath said will we do" (24:3). But they had done precisely what God had forbidden them to do. While Moses was on the mountaintop with God, the Israelites broke the first two commandments. And, according to James 2:10, when a person breaks one of the commandments, he is guilty of all. They had promised to keep the Law, but before they had received it in written form they had broken it.

Notice the words God used when He told Moses about the terrible sin of the people. God referred to the Israelites as "thy" people which "thou" (Moses) brought out of the land of Egypt (32:7). At this point, God was actually disclaiming the people of Israel. They had, by their sin, forfeited the right to all of His blessings. After they had made such a strong statement about being willing to do all that God said, they had utterly failed. And if God had treated them according to the Law which He had just spoken to them, they would have been lost beyond recovery and would have perished because of their own willful sin and apostasy.

Chapter 2

Moses Intercedes for Israel

In righteousness, God was ready to consume the Israelites. He said to Moses, "I have seen this people, and, behold, it is a stiffnecked people: now therefore let me alone, that my wrath may wax hot against them, and that I may consume them: and I will make of thee a great nation" (vv. 9,10).

The greatness of Moses is revealed here because he completely ignored God's offer to make of him a great nation. Moses began immediately to intercede for his people. Verses 11-13 record his intercession for them: "Lord, why doth thy wrath wax hot against thy people, which thou hast brought forth out of the land of Egypt with great power, and with a mighty hand?" (v. 11).

Whereas God had referred to the Israelites as "thy people" (v. 7) when talking to Moses, Moses referred to them as "thy people" (v. 11) when he talked with God. Moses refused to accept God's statement that they were his people, for he knew they belonged to the Lord. And Moses was absolutely right. All that had been done for the people had been done by God.

Moses was possibly the greatest intercessor who has ever lived, apart from the Lord Jesus Christ Himself. Moses' powerful intercession came at the time of his greatest test, for God was willing to make of him a great nation if Moses would let Him alone so He could wipe out the Israelites. God was willing to start all over again with one man. He had done this at the time of the flood when only Noah and his family had been spared. And now God was willing to destroy Israel and start all over with Moses.

17

On the surface, it is difficult to understand this passage, for it seems so unlike God to want to destroy the Israelites after bringing them into existence as a nation. I think the key to the passage, however, is that God was pleased with Moses' intercession and was really testing him to show us the type of man he was.

As Moses pleaded with God, he did not use his own close relationship to God as the basis of his appeal. Moses' thoughts were only of God and the Israelites, which indicated his genuine love for God and the people. Moses did not plead for that which would further his own cause temporarily, but he pleaded with eternal values in view. Moses had already made the decision to follow God by faith. Hebrews 11:24-26 says, "By faith Moses, when he was come to years, refused to be called the son of Pharaoh's daughter; choosing rather to suffer affliction with the people of God, than to enjoy the pleasures of sin for a season; esteeming the reproach of Christ greater riches than the treasures in Egypt: for he had respect unto the recompence of the reward."

Earlier Moses had refused to be called the son of Pharaoh's daughter; here he declined the offer to be made the head of a nation. He chose rather to be identified with the stiffnecked and disobedient Israelites. More than 40 years previously, he had chosen to go with them, and here he reaffirmed his choice.

In Moses we see a Christlike spirit. He did not seek his own glory, but he sought the best for others. Philippians 2:5-8 reveals that the Lord Jesus Christ laid aside personal glory to come to earth and shed His blood for the sin of mankind. This was unselfishness at its greatest!

Although Moses is not to be placed on the same level as the Lord Jesus Christ, he was selfless in his appeal to God not to destroy the Israelites and make of him a nation. The appeals of Moses had three bases: God's grace and mercy, God's glory and God's faithfulness.

Appeal to God's Grace and Mercy

Moses' appeal to God's grace and mercy is seen in Exodus 32:11: "Moses besought the Lord his God, and said, Lord, why doth thy wrath wax hot against thy people, which thou hast brought forth out of the land of Egypt with great power, and with a mighty hand?"

God had brought the Israelites out of Egypt by His grace, purely and simply. Everything God had done for the people, both in Egypt and after they left Egypt, was because of His grace. He had delivered them from Egypt by the Passover, He had brought them through the Red Sea, He had given them manna and meat to eat and water to drink in the wilderness, and He had fought for them against Amalek. All of this was simply because of His grace.

God had also extended much mercy to the Israelites. There is a distinction between grace and mercy. Grace is that which God gives to people because of who He is and what He is. He does not give to people because they are deserving but only because of His own person and character. Mercy is also given by God to people, but it is given when man deserves to be judged by God for sin. In His mercy, God makes provision for the sinfulness of man, although He does not overlook sin.

Moses made no effort to deny or to excuse Israel's sin. He knew God's grace had delivered Israel from bondage in Egypt, and he also seemed to be aware that where sin abounds, grace abounds much more (see Rom. 5:20). Moses knew that grace and mercy were part of God's character, so he pleaded on this basis.

Appeal to God's Glory

Moses also appealed on the basis of God's glory. Moses said, "Wherefore should the Egyptians speak, and say, For mischief did he bring them out, to slay them in the mountains, and to consume them from the face of the earth? Turn from thy fierce wrath, and repent of this evil against thy people" (Ex. 32:12).

Dealing with Israel's sin involved the character of God. If He spared the people, would they not think of Him as weak and consider His warnings and also His promises as nothing to be taken seriously? On the other hand, His glory was at stake if He destroyed them. To destroy the Israelites would bring great reproach on His name, especially from the Egyptians who knew He had taken them out of their land by miraculous power. If God destroyed the Israelites in the wilderness, it would give the enemy an occasion to boast over their destruction and to bring reproach on the name of God.

Just as at a later time God will gather the Israelites from among all nations for His name's sake (Ezek. 36:21-24), so He had brought the Israelites out of Egypt; and it was important that He preserve them for His name's sake.

This reveals to us two of the prime secrets in prevailing prayer. The first secret is bowing the heart to God's will, and the second secret is doing all to the glory of God. These two elements should always be found together in our lives. Whenever we accept something as God's will, we should also honor Him in all that we do. The Bible tells believers, "Whether therefore ye eat, or drink, or whatsoever ye do, do all to the glory of God" (I Cor. 10:31). This "do all" includes prayer.

Appeal to God's Faithfulness

Moses not only appealed on the basis of God's grace and mercy and on the basis of His glory but also on the basis of God's faithfulness. Moses said, "Remember Abraham, Isaac, and Israel, thy servants, to whom thou swarest by thine own self, and saidst unto them, I will multiply your seed as the stars of heaven, and all this land that I have spoken of will I give unto your seed, and they shall inherit it for ever" (Ex. 32:13).

God had made binding, unconditional promises, and Moses was reminding God of those promises. Notice that Moses used nothing in the lives of the Israelites as a basis for his pleading, for they had committed sin worthy of His wrath. Moses' plea was based on the character of God, particularly His faithfulness.

When God promised the land to Abraham, Isaac and Jacob, He had made unconditional agreements, or covenants, with them. God promised to do certain things whether individual descendants of Abraham responded favorably or not. So the fact that God told Moses He wanted to destroy the Israelites and make of Moses a new nation indicates that it was only a test of Moses.

Concerning God's promise to Abraham, the Book of Hebrews says, "For when God made promise to Abraham, because he could swear by no greater, he sware by himself. . . . Wherein God, willing more abundantly to shew unto the heirs of promise the immutability of his counsel, confirmed it by an oath: that by two immutable things, in which it was impossible for God to lie, we might have a strong consolation, who have fled for refuge to lay hold upon the hope set before us" (6:13,17,18).

Since God had bound Himself by His own Word, there was no greater basis for Moses' plea than the faithfulness of God. It would have been hopeless for Moses to have pleaded on the basis of what Israel was, because all that they were and did only exposed them to the righteous indignation of a holy God. Moses pleaded on the basis of God's faithfulness, because he knew that "God is not a man, that he should lie; neither the son of man, that he should repent: hath he said, and shall he not do it? Or hath he spoken, and shall he not make it good?" (Num. 23:19).

These considerations weighed so heavily on Moses that he refused to even think about the divine offer to make him the only survivor and the progenitor of a great nation. Speaking of this time in Israel's history, the psalmist wrote: "Therefore he said that he would destroy them, had not Moses his chosen stood before him in the breach, to turn away his wrath, lest he should destroy them" (Ps. 106:23). Remember, God had told Moses, "Let me alone, that my wrath may wax hot against them, and that I may consume them" (Ex. 32:10).

After Moses' great intercession for the people of Israel, "the Lord repented of the evil which he thought to do unto his people" (v. 14). These words do not mean that God changed His mind or altered His purpose, because with Him there is "no variableness, neither shadow of turning" (James 1:17). God never deviates even slightly from His eternal purpose.

When the Scriptures speak of God's "repenting," they are employing a figure of speech in language we can understand. As far as Moses was concerned, God seemingly changed His mind. The statement of Exodus 32:14 simply expresses in human terms the fact that God had answered Moses' prayer.

Moses' faith rose above all difficulties. He claimed God's help and—inasmuch as God cannot deny Himself—Moses' prayer was answered. It was answered because his intercession was based on the grace and mercy of God for His people, on the glory of God which was at stake, and on the faithfulness of God to His own Word.

The Mediator Becomes the Judge

The scene changed suddenly as Moses finished interceding for his people and received God's affirmative answer. "Moses turned, and went down from the mount, and the two tables of the testimony were in his hand: the tables were written on both their sides; on the one side and on the other were they written. And the tables were the work of God, and the writing was the writing of God, graven upon the tables" (Ex. 32:15,16).

As Moses and Joshua were on their way down the mountain, they heard the people shouting, and Joshua said, "There is a noise of war in the camp" (v. 17). But Moses and Joshua soon decided that the noise was not that of war but that the people were singing. "And it came to pass, as soon as he came nigh unto the camp, that he saw the calf, and the dancing: and Moses' anger waxed hot, and he cast the tables out of his hands, and brake them beneath the mount" (v. 19).

After his magnificent intercession before God, Moses came down the mountain and saw Israel's idolatry. He immediately agreed with God about the awfulness of the peoples' sin and began at once to pronounce judgment on them.

On the mountain, Moses was the typical mediator, pleading effectually before the Lord to turn away His wrath from His stiffnecked people. But at the foot of the mountain, as Moses viewed the idolatrous Israelites breaking the first two commandments, he threw down the tables of the Law in holy indignation. This was the same holy indignation which Moses had seen in God. He had been with God long enough that he expressed the very characteristics of God. Moses' wrath was not so much against the people as it was against their horrible sin of idolatry, which God had specifically forbidden.

After Moses threw down the tables of stone and broke them, "he took the calf which they had made, and burnt it in the fire, and ground it to powder, and strawed [scattered] it upon the water, and made the children of Israel drink of it" (v. 20). Then he publicly rebuked Aaron as the one responsible and, therefore, guilty of this most shameful act of idolatry. Moses asked Aaron, "What did this people unto thee, that thou hast brought so great a sin upon them?" (v. 21).

After rebuking Aaron for his part in this hideous sin, "Moses stood in the gate of the camp, and said, Who is on the Lord's side? Let him come unto me. And all the sons of Levi gathered themselves together unto him. And he said unto them, Thus saith the Lord God of Israel, Put every man his sword by his side, and go in and out from gate to gate throughout the camp, and slay every man his brother, and every man his companion, and every man his neighbor. And the children of Levi did according to the word of Moses: and there fell of the people that day about three thousand men" (vv. 26-28).

Notice the extreme contrast between the intercession and the judging. The contrast is so radical that many have been perplexed by it and have suggested many absurd explanations which are out of harmony with the overall incident as it is presented by the Scriptures. Sin against the person of God, as in all cases of idolatrous worship and practices, requires drastic measures. Judgment had to take place before the call to consecration.

So we learn that Moses, who so effectively interceded in behalf of the people and stopped the destroying hand of God, suddenly judged the people himself because of their sin.

Christ as Judge

The question that arises here is, Was Moses, in his judging, no longer the foreshadowing of Christ as our intercessor? The answer is yes—an emphatic yes.

On the mountain, he is seen as a type of Christ making intercession in behalf of his people. When God wanted to destroy the Israelites, Moses brought forth a threefold argument against such action. He appealed to the grace and mercy of God, to the glory of God and to the faithfulness of God. But when he came down from the mountain and saw firsthand how the people had sinned against the person of God, Moses acted as judge. Awful sin had been committed, and judgment had to fall on it.

In his hands Moses carried the tables of stone which declared that the righteous requirements of the Law cannot be set aside in any way. Sin had to be judged. Galatians 6:7 states the timeless principle: "Whatsoever a man soweth, that shall he also reap."

Notice what the Apostle John saw in his vision of the Lord Jesus Christ while on the Isle of Patmos: "I turned to see the voice that spake with me. And being turned, I saw seven golden candlesticks; and in the midst of the seven candlesticks one like unto the Son of man, clothed with a garment down to the foot, and girt about the paps [chest] with a golden girdle" (Rev. 1:12,13).

This is the way John saw the Lord Jesus Christ's appearing to the seven churches, because the seven candlesticks symbolized the seven churches (see v. 20). But the aspect of judgment could also be seen in the appearance of Christ: "His head and his hairs were white like wool, as white as snow; and his eyes were as a flame of fire; and his feet like unto fine brass, as if they burned in a furnace; and his voice as the sound of many waters. And he had in his right hand seven stars: and out of his mouth went a sharp twoedged sword: and his countenance was as the sun shineth in his strength" (vv. 14-16). So in these verses we see aspects of the character of Christ which judged—"eyes . . . as a flame of fire"; "feet like unto fine brass, as if they burned in a furnace"; and "out of his mouth went a sharp twoedged sword."

A true picture of Christ not only includes characteristics that reflect His love but also characteristics that reflect His judgment. He is both Saviour and intercessor, and He is a judge who cannot overlook sin. He Himself has borne the penalty for sin for the entire world (I John 2:2), and any person who wants to be delivered from condemnation must personally receive Jesus Christ as Saviour.

So as we consider Moses' actions, we see that he foreshadowed Jesus Christ even in the judging of sin. Just as

Moses, in holy indignation, threw down the tables of stone and shattered them (Ex. 32:19), so Jesus "went into the temple, and began to cast out them that sold and bought in the temple, and overthrew the tables of the moneychangers, and the seats of them that sold doves" (Mark 11:15). He said to the people, "Is it not written, My house shall be called of all nations the house of prayer? But ye have made it a den of thieves" (v. 17).

Prior to worshiping the golden calf, the Israelites had seen the great majesty and awesomeness of God when He spoke to them from the mountain. Six weeks later, while they could still see the evidence of God's awesome presence on the mountaintop as He spoke to Moses, they repudiated God and called for a substitute god. There was no other choice—judgment had to be exercised.

Moses Rebukes Aaron

What a contrast we see between Moses and Aaron! Aaron responded to Moses, "Let not the anger of my lord wax hot: thou knowest the people, that they are set on mischief. For they said unto me, Make us gods, which shall go before us: for as for this Moses, the man that brought us up out of the land of Egypt, we wot not what is become of him. And I said unto them, Whosoever hath any gold, let them break it off. So they gave it me: then I cast it into the fire, and there came out this calf" (Ex. 32:22-24).

Aaron had no sense of the terribleness of the sin he had just committed; there was no indication of repentance at this time. He accepted no blame himself but endeavored to place all the blame on others. How ridiculous of him to expect Moses to believe that he had just thrown the jewelry into the fire and the calf came out! He was like Adam and Eve in the Garden of Eden, who refused to accept personal responsibility for what had taken place.

Leaders in Christian circles so often claim they must make concessions because the people demand it. The life of Saul provides a good lesson concerning this matter. God told Saul to completely wipe out the remembrance of Amalek by destroying everyone and everything, but Saul was disobedient (see I Sam. 15:2-9). When Samuel faced him with this disobedience, Saul said, "The people spared the best of the sheep and of the oxen, to sacrifice unto the Lord thy God; and the rest we have utterly destroyed" (v. 15). This was Saul's excuse—he had made concessions because the people demanded it. But Samuel told him, "To obey is better than sacrifice" (v. 22).

Aaron was afraid of the people more than he was afraid of God. We all have this tendency; we seem to be more concerned about what people say than about what God's Word says on a given subject. It is important for every believer to fix his eyes on God and to obey Him, regardless of what people say.

Aaron could not stand up against a few people, but Moses feared God and walked so close to Him that he did not fear an army of over 600,000 Israelites (see Num. 1:46). Moses boldly proclaimed the execution of judgment on those who led in this sin.

The contrast between Aaron and Moses reveals the contrast between a servant of men and a servant of God. Each Christian should ask himself, Am I serving God, or am I only serving people? When a person acts with God, he always acts with power. The person who acts with men or because of fear of men, acts with weakness.

Not only did Aaron blame the others, but he also refused to take any personal responsibility. Not only that, he told an outright lie. He had fashioned the golden calf with a graving tool (Ex. 32:4), but he told Moses he had just thrown the jewelry in the fire, and the calf came out (v. 24).

If it had not been for the intercession of Moses, God would have destroyed Aaron for his responsibility in this terrible sin. In telling the people of this incident later, Moses said, "The Lord was very angry with Aaron to have destroyed him: and I prayed for Aaron also the same time" (Deut. 9:20).

No Neutrality

The Exodus account refers to the nakedness of the people: "When Moses saw that the people were naked; (for Aaron had made them naked unto their shame among their enemies:) then Moses stood in the gate of the camp, and said, Who is on the Lord's side?" (Ex. 32:25,26).

The people were naked because they had indulged in idolatrous sensualism, which accompanies idol worship. This called for drastic action. Thus, Moses asked the people who had not bowed their knee to the golden calf to take a stand as to whether they were on the Lord's side or not. Where there is open apostasy, there can be no neutrality. The Bible says, "What agreement hath the temple of God with idols? For ye are the temple of the living God; as God hath said, I will dwell in them, and walk in them; and I will be their God, and they shall be my people. Wherefore come out from among them, and be ye separate, saith the Lord, and touch not the unclean thing; and I will receive you" (II Cor. 6:16,17).

Hebrews 10 clearly reveals that there can be no neutrality where there is open apostasy. Verse 26 says, "For if we sin wilfully after that we have received the knowledge of the truth, there remaineth no more sacrifice for sins." Israel had sinned willfully; they knew the truth. God had mercifully and graciously delivered them from Egypt and had sustained them in the wilderness. They had seen God's miracle-working power on several occasions. But at the foot of Mount Sinai they sinned against all this knowledge.

To those who sin against knowledge, the Book of Hebrews says, "There remaineth no more sacrifice for sins, but a certain fearful looking for of judgment and fiery indignation, which shall devour the adversaries" (vv. 26,27). The writer of Hebrews was not referring to eternal condemnation but to physical judgment.

He went on to say, "He that despised Moses' law died without mercy under two or three witnesses" (v. 28). This is precisely what happened to the Israelites after they made the golden calf; Moses brought judgment on them.

Hebrews 10:30 says, "For we know him that hath said, Vengeance belongeth unto me, I will recompense, saith the Lord. And again, The Lord shall judge his people." And as a summary statement concerning any who would rebel against God, verse 31 says, "It is a fearful thing to fall into the hands of the living God."

Because there was open apostasy among the Israelites, Moses was concerned that there be no neutrality lest the vengeance of God come on them. Earlier, God had told Moses, "Let me alone, . . . that I may consume them" (Ex. 32:10). The judgment of God was suspended because of Moses' great intercession for the people. But as Moses saw the hideous sin with his own eyes, he was concerned that his judgment be exercised immediately, or else God might have still judged.

Physical Judgment

The judgment involved was not an eternal condemnation in hell; rather, it was a physical judgment for the sin they had committed. Sin cannot be overlooked, and those who had sinned suffered physical consequences because of it.

Moses wanted every person to take a definite stand for or against God; thus, he commanded, "Who is on the Lord's side? Let him come unto me" (v. 26).

Today, as we take our stand with the Lord, it is important to realize that we are not to fight people, we are to fight sin. Ephesians 6:12 tells believers, "For we wrestle not against flesh and blood, but against principalities, against powers, against the rulers of the darkness of this world, against spiritual wickedness in high places." Because our battle is not against flesh and blood, we are not to fight people. Our battle is against spiritual wickedness, so our real fight is against sin wherever it is found. The greatest means of fighting is by prayer against the evil forces that promote sin. What a shame it is when believers fight believers. Christians should be able to live in such harmony that the unsaved will be attracted to Christ as a result. Jesus said, "That they all may be one; as thou, Father, art in me, and I in thee, that they also may be one in us: that the world may believe that thou hast sent me" (John 17:21). The unity of believers is a convincing proof that God has sent Jesus Christ into the world to take care of the sin issue.

When Moses commanded the Israelites to take their stand for the Lord, "all the sons of Levi gathered themselves together unto him" (Ex. 32:26). To this group, Moses presented what must have amounted to the most severe test they had ever faced. He instructed them to kill those who had been guilty of worshiping the golden calf, most likely referring to the leaders in the sin. Apparently, there was no other remedy for cleansing Israel of this atrocious sin.

Hebrews 10:29 says, "Of how much sorer punishment, suppose ye, shall he be thought worthy, who hath trodden under foot the Son of God, and hath counted the blood of the covenant, wherewith he was sanctified, an unholy thing, and hath done despite unto the Spirit of grace?" This New Testament passage reveals what took place when the Israelites worshiped the golden calf. The Israelites had trodden under foot God Himself, who was even then on the mountaintop in the cloud. They could see the cloud of His glory, but they completely disregarded Him and even trod under foot the blood which had emancipated them from Egypt.

Aaron had told the people, "These be thy gods, O Israel, which brought thee up out of the land of Egypt" (Ex. 32:4). What a total disregard for the blood that had redeemed them! There was no alternative but to bring the severest of judgments on the people.

This may perplex some people, because it does not seem to harmonize with the love of God that the Bible speaks of. God is love (I John 4:8), yet that love demands righteous judgment. In addition to preaching the love of God, there also needs to be the preaching of the wrath of a holy God on all those who disown Him as Saviour and Lord.

Everyone will someday be forced to acknowledge Jesus Christ as Saviour and Lord. Philippians 2 says that Jesus Christ was willing to leave the glory He had with the Father and come to earth to die on the cross for the sin of the world (see vv. 5-8). "Wherefore God also hath highly exalted him, and given him a name which is above every name: that at the name of Jesus every knee should bow, of things in heaven, and things in earth, and things under the earth; and that every tongue should confess that Jesus Christ is Lord, to the glory of God the Father" (vv. 9-11).

During the coming Great Tribulation, people will endeavor to escape the wrath of God but will be unable to do so. "The kings of the earth, and the great men, and the rich men, and the chief captains, and the mighty men, and every bondman, and every free man, hid themselves in the dens and in the rocks of the mountains; and said to the mountains and rocks, Fall on us, and hide us from the face of him that sitteth on the throne, and from the wrath of the Lamb: for the great day of his wrath is come; and who shall be able to stand?" (Rev. 6:15-17). No wonder Hebrews 10:31 says, "It is a fearful thing to fall into the hands of the living God."

God cannot lower His standards for even one minute. Open repudiation of God, as seen in the worship of the golden calf, calls for open judgment of sin. The judgment resulted in the death of about 3000 men (Ex. 32:28).

Moses' Power and Authority

The people were terror-stricken and awed by the irrefutable power exercised by Moses. He stood, one man against more than 600,000 soldiers (Num. 1:46), and commanded that those who were guilty of this sin be put to death. Moses had just been in the very presence of God, and no one was able to resist his authority and power.

As the people viewed the threatening cloud on the mountaintop above them, revealing God's presence, they could offer no resistance, and 3000 were slain because they had repudiated God. Every person must have been weighed down—some with remorse for their sin, others with dread that the wrath of God would destroy even more of them. No doubt they were vividly reminded at this time of the great numbers of Egyptians who had been destroyed at the time of the Passover and in the Red Sea. Perhaps they wondered if they would suffer a similar fate in the desert. They undoubtedly remembered the awful voice of God which they had heard about six weeks earlier, specifically prohibiting them from making any graven images. They had been quick at that time to say they would do everything God commanded, but they had committed a terrible sin. They had not feared God as they should have.

Regrettably, we are living in similar days. Relatively few people fear God. People speak mockingly of an almighty God, and He may have to lash out in fury again to show them the seriousness of such sin. We who know the Lord Jesus Christ as Saviour possess the sword of the Spirit, and with it we must engage in spiritual warfare and smite the Enemy whenever he lifts his head against Christ. As has been indicated previously, we do this, not by attacking people, but by attacking sin wherever it is found. Ephesians 6:10-18 instructs believers concerning spiritual warfare. Because we live in days of apostasy, it is extremely important that we take this passage seriously and obey its instructions.

Some speak of Jesus Christ, but they actually deny the effectiveness of the blood of Christ which has provided salvation for mankind. Many, even in religious circles, deny the inerrancy of the Scriptures, the virgin birth of Christ, His substitutionary death, His resurrection from the dead and His personal return. These are the fundamentals of the faith, and anyone who denies them actually denies the foundational truths of Christianity.

There is also a sense, however, in which those who know Jesus Christ as Saviour can deny Him. By their actions, they can deny that they belong totally to God. The tendency today is for believers to become consumed with the materialistic philosophy of the age. Those who do so are guilty of worshiping the idol of materialism.

May those of us who know Jesus Christ as Saviour determine within our hearts to fix our eyes on Christ and to serve and honor Him, regardless of the apostasy that is everywhere about us. Remember Moses' searching question: "Who is on the Lord's side?" (Ex. 32:26).

Chapter 3

Moses' Greatest Moment

After the judgment of God had fallen on the leaders of those responsible for the golden-calf incident, Moses told the people, "Consecrate yourselves to day to the Lord, even every man upon his son, and upon his brother; that he may bestow upon you a blessing this day" (Ex. 32:29). Moses was concerned that the people separate themselves from all the contamination of sin so that God might bless them.

Moses' Intercession

The following day, Moses said to the people, "Ye have sinned a great sin: and now I will go up unto the Lord; peradventure I shall make an atonement for your sin" (v. 30). This gives us the background for what was probably Moses' greatest moment. At this time Moses made his unparalleled intercession for the people.

Notice that Moses was not absolutely sure he would be able to gain atonement for the people's sin. Moses said, "Peradventure [perhaps] I shall make an atonement for your sin" (v. 30). Moses put himself into the breach—between God and His people—in an endeavor to achieve atonement for the sin of the Israelites.

Scripture records no other intercession that parallels Moses' intercession for Israel. Of course, the Lord Jesus Christ—because He is God—intercedes on a higher level than any human being. But Moses' intercession superceded that of any other human being recorded in the Bible. The Apostle Paul's intercession for his fellow Israelites came near in greatness to Moses' great intercessory prayer, but I do not believe it was quite as great in its nature (see Rom. 9:1-5).

Moses' intercession was a beautiful foreshadowing of the atonement God has provided for the human race. Although mankind has been separated from God because of sin, God Himself made reconciliation possible by sending His only Son to pay the penalty for sin (John 3:16; Rom. 3:25). Because Moses loved the Israelites, he gave himself in interceding for them; because God loved mankind, He gave His only-begotten Son. Love and giving are inseparably linked—when one loves, he gives.

Through Moses, those who had led the people into the sin of idolatry had been punished, and the loyalty of the people had been reclaimed. There is, however, no record which indicates that the Israelites truly repented of their sin at that time. But they bent under the load of the terrible judgment, and Moses went before God to seek atonement for them.

In so doing, Moses was exercising his office of prophet—one who received a message from God and delivered it to the people. As their leader, Moses had a special relationship with the people, but he also had a special relationship to God. He spoke face to face with God concerning the people. What a relationship! It was as if Moses could feel the pulse of God's own heart.

I have often prayed that God would somehow break my own heart as His was broken for our sin. I want to feel the heartbeat of our great God who loved us so much He gave His only-begotten Son to die for our sins.

God's Righteousness and Mercy

As Moses was telling the people to wait while he went to meet God, God was on the mountaintop, as evidenced by the cloud. I can imagine God looking down and watching His servant Moses execute judgment on the people. Moses knew that God still waited in wrath on the mountain. This caused Moses to execute judgment with even greater urgency.

Remember, only part of the Law had been given at this time. But enough had been given that Moses knew a great deal about the horror of this terrible sin. He also knew about the uncompromising righteousness of an almighty God.

In the people's hearing, God had clearly stated, "Thou shalt have no other gods before me. Thou shalt not make unto thee any graven image, or any likeness of any thing that is in heaven above, or that is in the earth beneath, or that is in the water under the earth. Thou shalt not bow down thyself to them, nor serve them: for I the Lord thy God am a jealous God, visiting the iniquity of the fathers upon the children unto the third and fourth generation of them that hate me" (Ex. 20:3-5).

Although these verses list the prohibitions and judgment that would fall on those who disobeyed, verse 6 reveals God's mercy: "Shewing mercy unto thousands of them that love me, and keep my commandments." Even though many of God's people of Israel are still outside the fold of Jesus Christ, God is still showing mercy to them because of the love, compassion and faithfulness of Abraham. What a wonderful God He is!

But since God had said that He would visit the iniquity of the fathers to the third and fourth generations (v. 5), how could Moses' judgment suffice for the awful sin of idolatry? As severe as the judgment of Moses was, it was mild in comparison to the horrible sin that had been committed.

From experience, Moses knew that God had a way of atonement. In Egypt God had spared the life of the firstborn of all who had applied the blood of the substitute lamb. But what animal sacrifice would be sufficient to atone for the great sin of idolatry that the people had just committed? This sin was especially great because they had specific revelation indicating that they should not do it. They had sinned against their own knowledge.

Moses Offers Himself

When God had wanted to destroy the people for their sin, Moses had interceded for them. Moses pleaded on the basis of God's grace and mercy, His glory and His faithfulness. But now, Moses was entering into another aspect of intercession for the people. This intercession involved him specifically, and it involved a reinstatement of the Israelites as God's true people. God had told Moses, "Thy people, which thou broughtest out of the land of Egypt, have corrupted themselves" (32:7). God was not even claiming the people as His own at this point. Moses knew that the Israelites needed to be brought back into a relationship with God whereby He would claim them as His own and deal with them as His own.

For this reason, on the day after the leaders in the idolatry had been judged, "Moses said unto the people, Ye have sinned a great sin: and now I will go up unto the Lord; peradventure I shall make an atonement for your sin" (v. 30). One can imagine the mourning that took place among the Israelites because of the newly made graves—3000 of them. The awfulness of the sin of idolatry must have begun to pierce the hearts of the remaining Israelites. Surely they began to see the awesomeness of God on the mountain. The people must have been afraid of what judgment of God might fall on them next.

Think of all that Moses must have gone through between the day of judgment and the following day when he went to meet God. It was probably a sleepless night for him. His holy anger against this vile sin was probably followed by deep sorrow and pity for the people. No doubt his tears flowed freely during the night. His deepest compassions had been aroused. What love Moses had for his people!

By accepting previous sacrifices, God had indicated that He would accept an innocent substitute in the place of a just death for sin. He had also given part of the ceremonial law, so Moses would have had this underscored in his thinking.

But then came the great moment. Would God accept him—Moses—as the substitute for the sin of the people? Moses did not yet have the deep understanding of these matters as did the Apostle Paul, who wrote many centuries later. That is why I believe the intercession of Moses superceded that of Paul. Moses apparently did not clearly realize that man could not possibly make atonement for man. This is why he said, "Peradventure [perhaps] I shall make an atonement for your sin" (v. 30).

As Moses spoke to the people, he did not gloss over their gross wickedness; he did not attempt to minimize the awfulness of their sin. As he had earlier charged Aaron, he now—in deep love for God and for his people—charged them with the horribleness of their sin. He dealt with them faithfully about their sin, but he also referred to possible atonement.

Moses' hesitancy about whether or not atonement could be made for the people was undoubtedly a result of his concern over the enormity of their sin. Also, the people had given no indication that they had truly repented of their sin. Moses would have known that forgiveness could not be obtained without repentance for the sin.

In his announcement that he would go before the Lord in an endeavor to make atonement, Moses did not tell the people the price he was personally willing to pay—that of sacrificing himself as a substitute for their sin. But deeply locked in his own heart was that agony of love for them which caused him to be prepared to offer himself to God as a sacrifice for their sin.

It is evident that Moses intended to offer himself as a personal sacrifice for Israel's sin, because when he returned to God, he said, "Oh, this people have sinned a great sin, and have made them gods of gold. Yet now, if thou wilt forgive their sin—; and if not, blot me, I pray thee, out of thy book which thou hast written" (vv. 31,32). Moses was willing to be sent to hell for the people's sake if that could atone for their sin. What an offer!

Earlier, God had wanted Moses to step aside so He could consume the people for their sin, and Moses had pleaded with God not to do so. Now, Moses offered himself as a possible substitute sacrifice in behalf of the people. In effect, he said, "Let me die, if that will mean life for them. But if not, then destroy me too."

No doubt this secret was locked in Moses' heart as he climbed the mountain alone that day into the thick, foreboding cloud that was hiding God's presence. As he started up the mountain, probably with his head bowed, the people could see and begin to realize how much this man loved them. Imagine how the people felt as they stood watching and wondering what God would do. Would Moses be able to make atonement for them or not?

Notice the expression Moses used when he confessed his people's sin to God and asked for forgiveness: "If thou wilt forgive their sin—; and if not, blot me, I pray thee, out of thy book which thou hast written" (v. 32). As Moses thought of the alternative if God did not forgive the people of their sin, he could not even finish the sentence. The heart of God must have been moved toward His faithful servant, for this proposal would have reminded Him of another scene that would occur approximately 1500 years later when His own Son would die on the cross for mankind.

Moses' Offer Rejected

Moses soon discovered that his offer could not be accepted by God. No one who has a sin nature can atone for the sins of another. Psalm 49:7 says, "None of them can by any means redeem his brother, nor give to God a ransom for him." Moses himself was a sinner; he had even murdered someone years before. He needed atonement for his own sins, so he was in no position to atone for the sins of others.

God's answer to Moses was clear: "Whosoever hath sinned against me, him will I blot out of my book" (Ex. 32:33). There is no indication that God said this in a harsh way; rather, God must have looked on Moses with love and compassion. But God made it clear to Moses that he could not atone for the sin of the people; rather, whoever sinned would pay the consequences.

Many centuries later another person made a similar request. Concerning his fellow Israelites, the Apostle Paul said, "I say the truth in Christ, I lie not, my conscience also bearing me witness in the Holy Ghost, that I have great heaviness and continual sorrow in my heart. For I could wish that myself were accursed from Christ for my brethren, my kinsmen according to the flesh" (Rom. 9:1-3). But this was not possible for Paul, just as it was not possible for Moses.

As Moses received further revelation from God about sin and laws concerning sacrifice, he would clearly understand why it was not possible for him to make atonement for the Israelites. The blood sacrifices of the Old Testament pointed to the time when the Lord Jesus Christ would enter the human race and become *the* sacrifice for sin. This is why John the Baptist exclaimed concerning Christ: "Behold the Lamb of God, which taketh away the sin of the world" (John 1:29).

The sin of the entire human race was placed on Christ as He hung on the cross; thus II Corinthians 5:21 says, "For he hath made him to be sin for us, who knew no sin; that we might be made the righteousness of God in him." Because He was God as well as man, the Lord Jesus Christ was able to pay the penalty for the sin of the entire human race. No other person could have done this, because all except Christ were born with a sin nature. This is why Acts 4:12 says, "Neither is there salvation in any other: for there is none other name under heaven given among men, whereby we must be saved."

The provision for the payment of the penalty of sin was made entirely because of the grace and mercy of God. The great question since the fall of man had revolved around how God would be propitiated, or satisfied, for the sin of man. God Himself solved the problem by sending His own Son to be that satisfaction for sin.

Romans 3:25 refers to this act of God's grace and mercy when it says concerning the Lord Jesus Christ, "Whom God hath set forth to be a propitiation through faith in his blood, to declare his righteousness for the remission of sins that are past, through the forbearance of God." First John 2:2 also refers to Christ's satisfying the demands of the Heavenly Father for the sins of mankind: "He is the propitiation for our sins: and not for our's only, but also for the sins of the whole world."

Because the Lord Jesus Christ has satisfied the Heavenly Father concerning sin, He alone was able to say, "I am the way, the truth, and the life: no man cometh unto the Father, but by me" (John 14:6).

The seriousness of rejecting this one way of salvation is seen in what Peter told the Israelites on the Day of Pentecost: "For Moses truly said unto the fathers, A prophet shall the Lord your God raise up unto you of your brethren, like unto me; him shall ye hear in all things whatsoever he shall say unto you. And it shall come to pass, that every soul, which will not hear that prophet, shall be destroyed from among the people" (Acts 3:22,23). How significant that Peter quoted Moses, who had offered himself as an atonement for the sin of Israel.

Even though no human could atone for the sin of others, "when the fulness of the time was come, God sent forth his Son, made of a woman, made under the law, to redeem them that were under the law, that we might receive the adoption of sons" (Gal. 4:4,5).

The Prophet Isaiah predicted the coming of the Lord Jesus Christ and all that He would endure for mankind. Isaiah prophesied: "Surely he hath borne our griefs, and carried our sorrows: yet we did esteem him stricken, smitten of God, and afflicted. But he was wounded for our transgressions, he was bruised for our iniquities: the chastisement of our peace was upon him; and with his stripes we are healed. All we like sheep have gone astray; we have turned every one to his own way; and the Lord hath laid on him the iniquity of us all.

"He was oppressed, and he was afflicted, yet he opened not his mouth: he is brought as a lamb to the slaughter, and as a sheep before her shearers is dumb, so he openeth not his mouth.

"Yet it pleased the Lord to bruise him; he hath put him to grief: when thou shalt make his soul an offering for sin, he shall see his seed, he shall prolong his days, and the pleasure of the Lord shall prosper in his hand. He shall see of the travail of his soul, and shall be satisfied: by his knowledge shall my righteous servant justify many; for he shall bear their iniquities" (Isa. 53:4-7,10,11). God was satisfied. God accepted the offering of the Lord Jesus Christ!

As Moses pleaded with God after the incident of the golden calf, he did not have all of this revelation concerning redemption and the Person of Christ. Without a doubt this is why this intercession was Moses' greatest moment. What tremendous love Moses had for his fellow Israelites—none greater was found until Christ Himself came to reveal God's love to a world of sinners.

God Sends an Angel

Although at first the Israelites were threatened with the loss of the divine presence, God offered to send His angel before them to lead them into the land of promise. God told Moses, "Therefore now go, lead the people unto the place of which I have spoken unto thee: behold, mine Angel shall go before thee" (Ex. 32:34). Although those responsible for sin would suffer for their sin, God conceded to send His angel to lead them on their way.

The reason God chose to send an angel rather than leading the Israelites by His own presence is indicated in Exodus 33:1-3: "And the Lord said unto Moses, Depart, and go up hence, thou and the people which thou hast brought up out of the land of Egypt, unto the land which I sware unto Abraham, to Isaac, and to Jacob, saying, Unto thy seed will I give it: and I will send an angel before thee; and I will drive out the Canaanite, the Amorite, and the Hittite, and the Perizzite, the Hivite, and the Jebusite: unto a land flowing with milk and honey: for I will not go up in the midst of thee; for thou art a stiffnecked people: lest I consume thee in the way."

Moses had secured the Israelites' immediate safety as well as a promise of angelic guidance and protection. But these words of God make it clear that further chastisement was destined for the people because of their sin. No doubt this was because the offenders had shown no evidence of genuine repentance.

Although Moses had wanted to be a substitute for the people's sin, God had told him, "Whosoever hath sinned against me, him will I blot out of my book" (32:33). Even after promising an angel to guide them, God said, "Nevertheless in the day when I visit I will visit their sin upon them" (v. 34). Then God told them, "For I will not go up in the midst of thee; for thou art a stiffnecked people: lest I consume thee in the way" (33:3). Since there had been no evidence of repentance on the people's part, they had not yet been restored to fellowship in their covenant relationship with God. God's righteousness could not allow Him to personally guide the people because of their sin.

God's Chastening and Israel's Contrition

Moses' intercession had averted the penal wrath of God, but because of the lack of repentance and confession, the governmental consequences of their sin had not yet been removed. The people still needed to appropriate God's restoring mercy and grace. Because there had been no repentance, "the Lord plagued the people, because they made the calf, which Aaron made" (Ex. 32:35).

This incident should remind those of us living in the 20th century that if it were not for the mercy of God, we would be consumed. His standards are much higher than we are ever able to attain on our own. If He so chose, He could destroy us because of our sin. Jeremiah realized this also, and he wrote: "But this I recall, therefore have I hope and expectation: it is of the Lord's mercies and loving-kindnesses that we are not consumed, because His (tender) compassions fail not. They are new every morning; great and abundant is Your stability and faithfulness. . . . For the Lord will not cast off for ever! But, though He causes grief, yet will He be moved to compassion according to the multitude of His lovingkindnesses and tender mercies. For He does not willingly and from His heart afflict or grieve the children of men" (Lam. 3:21-23, 31-33, Amplified).

God does not afflict people because He delights to do so; He afflicts because of a special purpose. Hebrews 12:10 clearly reveals that God afflicts us "for our profit, that we might be partakers of his holiness." The afflicting, or chastening, is not enjoyable at the time, but it produces that which is for our best and for God's glory. Verse 11 says, "Now no chastening for the present seemeth to be joyous, but grievous: nevertheless afterward it yieldeth the peaceable fruit of righteousness unto them which are exercised thereby."

Moses had been directed by the Lord to return to the camp with God's message for the people. Moses told them that God would not go up with them Himself, or He would consume them in the way because they were stiffnecked. "When the people heard these evil tidings, they mourned: and no man did put on him his ornaments" (Ex. 33:4).

Even the leaving off of their ornaments was because of the instruction of God: "For the Lord had said unto Moses, Say unto the children of Israel, Ye are a stiffnecked people: I will come up into the midst of thee in a moment, and consume thee: therefore now put off thy ornaments from thee, that I may know what to do unto thee. And the children of Israel stripped themselves of their ornaments by the mount Horeb" (vv. 5,6).

God's word, as delivered through Moses, brought a determined effect on the people. They were made to see the awfulness of their sin. They were brought low, into a state of contrition; repentance and worship were soon to follow. And because repentance was anticipated, the personal, divine presence of God was to be restored to them once they were fully brought into proper relationship with God. But only the fervent intercession of Moses for the people spared them from the righteous anger of God.

Had it not been for Moses' intercession, the people would have been exterminated. This is a beautiful foreshadowing of the Lord Jesus Christ, who now appears in the presence of the Father to intercede in behalf of all believers. Not only does He intercede, but "he is able also to save them to the uttermost that come unto God by him, seeing he ever liveth to make intercession for them" (Heb. 7:25). Because the Lord Jesus Christ is eternal and does not die as the Old Testament priests did, He is able to make intercession for believers forever.

Apart from the intercessory work of the Lord Jesus Christ, we would not be able to survive the holy wrath of God. Jesus Christ pleads our case before God on the merits of His own atoning sacrifice in our behalf. This intercessory ministry of Jesus sustains us in our pilgrim journey on the earth. Hebrews 9:24 says, "For Christ is not entered into the holy places made with hands, which are the figures of the true; but into heaven itself, now to appear in the presence of God for us."

Thus we see that Israel was not consumed, but they were plagued because of their lack of repentance. Unfortunately, there is little emphasis on repentance today. The Lord Jesus Christ said, "Except ye repent, ye shall all likewise perish" (Luke 13:3). The Lord Jesus also told the Church of Ephesus, "Remember therefore from whence thou art fallen, and repent, and do the first works; or else I will come unto thee quickly, and will remove thy candlestick out of his place, except thou repent" (Rev. 2:5).

God pronounced Israel a stiffnecked people, and this required that they be humbled. The first hopeful sign of their repentance is recorded in Exodus 33:4. After they heard God's message, "they mourned: and no man did put on him his ornaments." To "mourn" means to "sorrow" or to "lament." This was the first sign of their repentance. But true repentance is more than sorrow; it is a change of mind about one's sin and about God. Those who recognize their sinful condition and believe in Jesus Christ as Saviour have repented and receive forgiveness of sin and eternal life.

When the Israelites learned that Jehovah Himself would not accompany them to the Promised Land, they were moved to deep contrition. How could they go on without Him? Their eyes were opened, and they saw the seriousness of their sin.

Their situation was so different from that of the Church of Laodicea, to whom the Lord Jesus Christ said, "I know thy works, that thou art neither cold nor hot: I would thou wert cold or hot. So then because thou art lukewarm, and neither cold nor hot, I will spue thee out of my mouth" (Rev. 3:15,16).

This church, which had a nature similar to conditions that will exist at the end of the Church Age, prided itself in its own possessions and accomplishments. However, Christ told this church that it did not realize that it was "wretched, and miserable, and poor, and blind, and naked" (v. 17).

Jesus invited this church to come to Him to have its needs fulfilled. He said, "Behold, I stand at the door, and knock: if any man hear my voice, and open the door, I will come in to him, and will sup with him, and he with me" (v. 20). This verse is commonly used in talking with unsaved people, but these words were spoken by Christ to a church that had put Him on the outside. He was willing to come in to them and have fellowship with them if only they would invite Him to do so.

What is it like in your church? Has Christ been put on the outside? If so, He wants to come inside to have fellowship with believers. How sad that Christians can be so busy in the "work of the Lord" that they actually keep Christ on the outside as far as fellowship with Him is concerned. We have fellowship with Him as we study His Word, meditate on it and talk to Him in prayer. If we are too busy to do these things, we are obviously busier than the Lord ever intended us to be.

As you endeavor to commune with God, does it sometimes seem that He is far away? Does it seem as if you cannot contact Him—as if your prayers get no farther than the ceiling? No doubt every believer experiences this feeling at times. But we can learn a valuable lesson about this matter from God's relationship to Israel.

A Special Tent

After the indication of repentance by the Israelites, "Moses took the tabernacle, and pitched it without the camp, afar off from the camp, and called it the Tabernacle of the congregation. And it came to pass, that every one which sought the Lord went out unto the tabernacle of the congregation, which was without the camp" (Ex. 33:7).

Although God had pronounced judgment on the people because of their sin, He also provided a way of escape. God had refused to come into the midst of the people lest He destroy them because of their sin, but He made it possible for them to go outside of the camp to meet Him. Where sin abounded, grace abounded much more (Rom. 5:20). As Romans 5:21 says, "That as sin hath reigned unto death, even so might grace reign through righteousness unto eternal life by Jesus Christ our Lord."

The "tabernacle" mentioned in Exodus 33 was a special tent, not the tabernacle mentioned in Exodus 25—31. This special tent was placed far outside the camp where those who wished to commune with God could do so. God had been openly repudiated by the people when they committed the gross sin of idolatry. Because of His holiness, He could not enter their midst without destroying them, but they could approach Him outside the camp. The tent represented God's abiding presence, and the people were able to meet Him there. This was an extension of God's grace. Before He punished them for sin, He furnished them with another opportunity for repentance. He waited outside the camp to see how they would respond.

The people availed themselves of God's forbearance. They were humbled by their sin and awed by the pronouncement of imminent destruction. In Egypt the Israelites were delivered from losing their firstborn by being sheltered beneath the blood; at Mount Sinai they were invited by God to come outside the camp to meet Him and thereby escape destruction.

Why was God's action so extreme at this time in comparison to the other times when the Israelites sinned? Although the people were guilty of sinning by murmuring against the leadership of Moses and the goodness of God, they had never before replaced God and disowned Him as they had by building and worshiping the golden calf. In fact, they even praised the golden calf as the one that had led them out of Egypt (32:4). Although God had delivered them, they rejected Him.

What a vivid reminder this is of the Lord Jesus Christ who "came unto his own, and his own received him not" (John 1:11). The Lord Jesus Christ was rejected by the very people He came to save. Just as God moved outside the camp of the Israelites, so also Jesus, "that he might sanctify the people with his own blood, suffered without the gate" (Heb. 13:12).

Jesus was crucified outside the gate of Jerusalem, but by shedding His blood on the cross, He provided salvation for all who would believe in His finished work of redemption. Because of what He has done for us, "let us go forth therefore unto him without the camp, bearing his reproach" (v. 13).

God calls for believers to separate themselves from those who deny Him if they are to have fellowship with Him. We must be willing to leave others and go outside the camp to Him. This is not a separation from other believers who may think differently than we do; it is a separation from those who deny the Lord. We are not to separate ourselves from other believers: "Not forsaking the assembling of ourselves together, as the manner of some is; but exhorting one another: and so much the more, as ye see the day approaching" (10:25).

The Bible makes it clear that believers are not to be under the control of unbelievers. "Be ye not unequally yoked together with unbelievers: for what fellowship hath righteousness with unrighteousness? And what communion hath light with darkness? And what concord hath Christ with Belial? Or what part hath he that believeth with an infidel? And what agreement hath the temple of God with idols? For ye are the temple of the living God; as God hath said, I will dwell in them, and walk in them; and I will be their God, and they shall be my people. Wherefore come out from among them, and be ye separate, saith the Lord, and touch not the unclean thing; and I will receive you" (II Cor. 6:14-17).

God Meets Moses

Notice what happened after Moses moved the tent outside the camp. "It came to pass, when Moses went out unto the tabernacle, that all the people rose up, and stood every man at his tent door, and looked after Moses, until he was gone into the tabernacle" (Ex. 33:8). Why were the people watching so intently? Apparently they were wondering whether they had sinned away their last opportunity or whether God would actually meet Moses, which would be an indication that He would meet with them.

"It came to pass, as Moses entered into the tabernacle, the cloudy pillar descended, and stood at the door of the tabernacle, and the Lord talked with Moses" (v. 9). The Lord met Moses! There was still hope for them! Even this gracious manifestation of God encouraged the people to repent.

Romans 2:4 states the timeless principle that "the goodness of God leadeth thee to repentance."

The Bible reveals that all who come to the Lord will not be cast out (John 6:37), but they must come to Him. This is why it was necessary for the Israelites to go outside of the camp individually to meet the Lord. "He that covereth his sins shall not prosper: but whoso confesseth and forsaketh them shall have mercy" (Prov. 28:13). Wholehearted repentance had to occur before there could be true worship of God.

The Bible clearly reveals that God extends grace and mercy to those who call on Him. God has said, "If my people, which are called by my name, shall humble themselves, and pray, and seek my face, and turn from their wicked ways; then will I hear from heaven, and will forgive their sin" (II Chron. 7:14).

Notice the response of the Israelites after they realized that God had met Moses in the tabernacle: "All the people saw the cloudy pillar stand at the tabernacle door: and all the

people rose up and worshipped, every man in his tent door"
(Ex. 33:10). The worship of the true God was reinstated,
which indicated that the worship of the false god had been
repudiated.

Chapter 4

Moses' Spiritual Excellence

Moses had attained the highest pinnacle in his prayer life and in his fellowship with God. God could completely trust His servant. Because of Moses' intercession, God had even spared the lives of about three million people. Judgment had been meted out, but God spared the lives of the people of Israel, and they were restored to fellowship with Him.

All of this stirred up Moses' inner heart so that he desired an even more intimate relationship with God. Perhaps you wonder how he could desire more since he already had so much. Yet, as long as the believer lives he should continue to grow in his personal relationship with the Lord. However, many believers seem to be content with only salvation. They have been delivered from condemnation by trusting Jesus Christ as Saviour, and they seem to spend the rest of their time enjoying themselves and the things of this world. This is shallow Christianity. We are to enjoy ourselves, but we are to find our enjoyment in God, not in the things of this world.

Moses' Relationship With God

The special relationship Moses had with God is recorded in Exodus 33:11: "The Lord spake unto Moses face to face, as a man speaketh unto his friend." This relationship was different from that enjoyed by any other person in the Old Testament. Rather than revealing Himself to Moses by visions, in dreams or through an angel, God revealed Himself directly to Moses.

The relationship which Moses had with God has been surpassed only by the Lord Jesus when He was on earth, but, of course, He was the God-Man. No other mere human being had a relationship with God such as Moses had.

The closeness that Moses had with God was not attained by special merits or because God was partial to him. Rather, it was a matter of spiritual growth over many years. In fact, Moses was well over 80 years of age, and he had been growing spiritually since he was 40. At that time he had made the decision mentioned in Hebrews 11:24-26: "By faith Moses, when he was come to years, refused to be called the son of Pharaoh's daughter; choosing rather to suffer affliction with the people of God, than to enjoy the pleasures of sin for a season; esteeming the reproach of Christ greater riches than the treasures in Egypt: for he had respect unto the recompence of the reward."

During the next 40 years Moses was on the backside of the desert, learning in the "school" of God. This brought him into a closer relationship with God, because they had contact on a daily and personal basis. Moses must have climbed Mount Sinai many times to be alone with God. After God had trained Moses during these years and had strengthened his faith through experience for at least a year in Egypt, Moses took over the leadership of this great people, the nation of Israel.

It was to Moses' credit that he did not compromise as he led the Israelites. He also had a holy boldness in the matter of prayer as he led the people. Meeting God alone made Moses the leader he was. His frequent meetings alone with God were the key to his life.

As we spend time alone with God, He will be able to entrust us with greater things also. But in order for God to trust us with significant responsibilities, we must become trustworthy. As we develop a greater reliance on God and spend more time with Him, He can trust us with more because we then know Him better.

As Moses spent time alone with God, he not only interceded for the Israelites but also came to have such a deep spiritual sense of concern that he was even willing to give himself to atone for their sin. This reveals a heart that was near to God's own heart. At one time God had asked Moses to leave Him alone so He could destroy the people, but Moses had continued to intercede, and the people were

spared. Moses understood the heart of God because he had
spent much time alone with Him.

Numbers 12 also reveals the type of relationship Moses
had with God. Moses' sister and brother—Miriam and
Aaron—complained because of the position of leadership
Moses had over them. The Bible says, "(Now the man Moses
was very meek, above all the men which were upon the face
of the earth)" (v. 3). The word "meek" does not mean that
Moses had a weak character; rather, it refers to strength
under control.

The close relationship of Moses and the Lord is evidenced
by what the Lord said at this time: "The Lord spake
suddenly unto Moses, and unto Aaron, and unto Miriam,
Come out ye three unto the tabernacle of the congregation.
And they three came out. . . . And he said, Hear now my
words: If there be a prophet among you, I the Lord will
make myself known unto him in a vision, and will speak unto
him in a dream. My servant Moses is not so, who is faithful in
all mine house. With him will I speak mouth to mouth, even
apparently, and not in dark speeches; and the similitude of
the Lord shall he behold: wherefore then were ye not afraid
to speak against my servant Moses?" (vv. 4,6-8).

Moses Seeks God's Glory

A study of Moses' life shows that he sought the glory of
God. As he prayed concerning the people, God granted his
request in various stages. As Moses received one thing from
the Lord, he asked for more and received more. God was not
reluctant to answer Moses' prayer, because Moses' prayers
were not motivated by self. Moses' whole concern was that
God might be glorified.

The prayers of Moses became bolder as he grew to know
the Lord better and had an even closer relationship with Him.
God was not giving in grudgingly to Moses' prayers; He really
wanted to do these things for His people, and Moses dared to
believe Him for what He could do. Moses dared to ask God to
work mightily in behalf of the people.

God is also looking today for people who will dare to
believe Him for mighty things. It is not necessary to be well
known by others or to know everything in the Bible, but it is

important to believe God for what He wants to do. God is looking for those He can trust as He did Moses. God has promised to work through those who call on Him for their strength. Jeremiah 33:3 says, "Call unto me, and I will answer thee, and shew thee great and mighty things, which thou knowest not." The Apostle Paul said that God "is able to do exceeding abundantly above all that we ask or think, according to the power that worketh in us" (Eph. 3:20).

Moses truly became God's man to the people. He was a prophet who gave them the message of God. In delivering God's message, Moses also executed judgment on those guilty of sin. Moses did not compromise God's standards or his own standards. On the other hand, Moses was quick in moving to secure God's mercy for the people.

After the leaders in the sin of idolatry had been killed, Moses pitched a tent outside the camp so the people could go there to meet God. Moses wanted the people to know that God would meet them if they responded and went outside the camp to meet Him. If God had gone within the camp, He would have destroyed the people for their wickedness. But His mercy allowed Him to meet the Israelites outside the camp.

God granted Moses' requests in various stages. First, God agreed to spare the people after Moses' intercession for them. "The Lord repented of the evil which he thought to do unto his people" (Ex. 32:14). God refused to personally lead the people to the Promised Land, but after Moses prayed again, God agreed to send an angel to lead them (v. 34).

But Moses was still not satisfied. After he had pitched the tent outside the camp so the people could meet God there, Moses went before the Lord with another petition. Moses said to Him, "See, thou sayest unto me, Bring up this people: and thou hast not let me know whom thou wilt send with me. Yet thou hast said, I know thee by name, and thou hast also found grace in my sight. Now therefore, I pray thee, if I have found grace in thy sight, shew me now thy way, that I may know thee, that I may find grace in thy sight: and consider that this nation is thy people" (33:12,13). Notice that Moses told God that the Israelites were "thy people."

As Moses talked with God, God gave him a wonderful promise: "My presence shall go with thee, and I will give thee rest" (v. 14). God agreed to spare the people and to personally lead them to the Promised Land.

The Lord also told Moses, "I will do this thing also that thou hast spoken: for thou hast found grace in my sight, and I know thee by name" (v. 17). The Lord's agreement to "do this thing also" was His agreement to personally lead the Israelites as Moses requested. What an answer to prayer! As a result of Moses' prayer, God Himself agreed to lead the Israelites to the Promised Land.

Moses' Bold Request

Having succeeded in receiving several answers to his prayers, Moses then evidenced his greatest boldness in what he requested of God. Moses said, "I beseech thee, shew me thy glory" (v. 18). Moses had been so encouraged by God's answers to his prayers that he sought for the ultimate. The one desire that burned within Moses was to know God better. There is a tremendous need for each believer to have this same desire.

Paul expressed his desire in these words: "That I may know him, and the power of his resurrection, and the fellowship of his sufferings, being made conformable unto his death" (Phil. 3:10). Peter said, "According as his divine power hath given unto us all things that pertaineth unto life and godliness, through the knowledge of him that hath called us to glory and virtue" (II Pet. 1:3).

In Paul's letter to the Ephesians, he recorded his prayers that apply to all believers: "That the God of our Lord Jesus Christ, the Father of glory, may give unto you the spirit of wisdom and revelation in the knowledge of him: the eyes of your understanding being enlightened; that ye may know what is the hope of his calling, and what the riches of the glory of his inheritance in the saints, and what is the exceeding greatness of his power to us-ward who believe, according to the working of his mighty power" (Eph. 1:17-19).

Paul also prayed, "That Christ may dwell in your hearts by faith; that ye, being rooted and grounded in love, may be able to comprehend with all saints what is the breadth, and length, and depth, and height; and to know the love of

Christ, which passeth knowledge, that ye might be filled with all the fulness of God" (3:17-19).

As the believer walks in close communion with God, there is always the desire to know Him better. If this is not the desire of the believer, something is seriously lacking in his spiritual life.

To Moses' request, "Shew me thy glory" (Ex. 33:18), God said, "I will make all my goodness pass before thee, and I will proclaim the name of the Lord before thee; and will be gracious to whom I will be gracious, and will shew mercy on whom I will shew mercy" (v. 19).

God's Glory

Verse 19 reveals that God's glory is seen in His goodness, or it could also be said that His glory is His goodness. Have you ever really considered what is involved in the goodness of the Lord? Someone has said, "His goodness is what He is in Himself." The sum total of His personal excellency is what He is and what He does. The only way we can really know Him and His glory today is to know what He does.

God also indicated to Moses that His glory is seen in His name: "I will proclaim the name of the Lord before thee" (v. 19). The Hebrew word translated "Lord" in this verse is the one from which "Jehovah" is derived. The word is related to what God told Moses earlier when He revealed Himself as "I Am That I Am" (3:14). This expression, as well as the name "Jehovah," reveals God as the ever-present One.

This was the God that Moses learned to know at the burning bush after he had spent 40 years in His wilderness school. There Moses learned much about the character of God.

Knowing the glory of God is seeing what God does because of His goodness. Exodus 34:6,7 says, "The Lord passed by before him, and proclaimed, The Lord, The Lord God, merciful and gracious, longsuffering, and abundant in goodness and truth, keeping mercy for thousands, forgiving iniquity and transgression and sin, and that will by no means clear the guilty; visiting the iniquity of the fathers upon the children, and upon the children's children, unto the third and to the fourth generation." These verses correspond with

Exodus 33:19—the same Hebrew word for "Lord" is used in both references.

Having told Moses that He would make His goodness pass before him, God said, "Thou canst not see my face: for there shall no man see me, and live. And the Lord said, Behold, there is a place by me, and thou shalt stand upon a rock: and it shall come to pass, while my glory passeth by, that I will put thee in a clift of the rock, and will cover thee with my hand while I pass by: and I will take away mine hand, and thou shalt see my back parts: but my face shall not be seen" (33:20-23).

God is spirit, so no one is actually able to see Him. If a person could see God, he would be unable to stand the awesomeness of His glory. Thus, even Moses was able to see God only by what He is and by what He does. In effect, God was telling Moses, "I can't show you My face, because if I did, you would not live. But I will show you my goodness, which reveals who I am and what I do." God was going to reveal Himself to Moses by showing His grace and mercy to him.

Grace and Mercy

Notice that God said, "I . . . will be gracious to whom I will be gracious, and will shew mercy on whom I will shew mercy" (Ex. 33:19). As discussed previously, the words "grace" and "mercy" are not synonymous; they are not used interchangeably. Grace is God's unmerited favor—favor which He bestows on mankind in spite of the fact that man deserves condemnation. Mercy follows grace, and it emphasizes God's seeing man in his pitiful condition and doing something to deliver him. Mercy always follows grace.

All the way from Egypt to Sinai, God had dealt with the Israelites on the basis of grace. They did not deserve any favors from God. In fact, they deserved exactly the opposite. Even though God had shown them so many favors, they murmured and complained again and again. Finally, they even repudiated God's leadership and asked Aaron to make gods to lead them. The Israelites certainly deserved the condemnation of God for repudiating His grace.

But then mercy was added to grace. God had pity on them in their miserable situation and did not destroy all of them, even though the leaders in the sin were destroyed.

In this incident, God made known something of His nature which had never been revealed to the people in depth—He made known His mercy. Mercy is one of His attributes, and when He extended mercy, He acted from Himself and of Himself. He extends mercy to whomever He chooses (v. 19). Mercy is the wonderful provision of God to meet the desperate need of the person who has failed to respond to His grace.

Since God is just, He must mete out a penalty on sin. Thus, justice and mercy met at Calvary. On the cross, the Lord Jesus Christ bore the sin of the world so that the penalty was paid. This, in turn, allowed God to extend mercy to all.

An interesting study of grace and mercy is found in Psalm 105 and 106. Psalm 105 gives the history of grace, and mercy is not once mentioned. But Psalm 106 tells the history of God's mercy, and the sin of Israel is frequently mentioned. Notice especially Psalm 106:4,5: "Remember me, O Lord, with the favor that thou bearest unto thy people: O visit me with thy salvation; that I may see the good of thy chosen, that I may rejoice in the gladness of thy nation, that I may glory with thine inheritance." Mercy is that wonderful quality of God's nature which meets the deep and desperate need of those who have sinned against His grace.

God's grace extends to us because we are worthless, empty and without hope in this world. But He extends His mercy to us because we are sinful and wicked. He can extend His mercy only because of the sacrifice of His Son, who shed His blood to pay the penalty for our sin. Thus, we are to come to the throne of grace to obtain mercy (Heb. 4:16).

Exodus 33:19 reveals that a person should not presume upon the mercy of God. God said, "I . . . will shew mercy on whom I will shew mercy." No one can claim mercy as a right. If that were the case, it would no longer be mercy. Moses prayed as no other man has prayed for his people and their needs. He obtained mercy for those he loved, and in so doing, he was able to behold the glory of God. Moses saw the wonderful grace of God extended to Israel in their experiences from Egypt to Sinai. Then, when Israel repudiated God, Moses was able to obtain mercy for them from God. God did not have to extend His mercy, but in Moses' greatest hour of intercession he obtained it for them from God. This, then, is the manner in which Moses beheld the glory of God. "And he [God] said, I will make all my goodness pass before thee, and I will proclaim the name of the Lord before thee" (v. 19).

Dealing With Sin

Today people have many different opinions about what it means to see the glory of God. Some think this means having a vision, and some talk about seeing Christ in the clouds or standing by their bedside. But when Moses asked to see the glory of the Lord, he was shown God's goodness. It was as if God were saying, "My glory is my goodness—what I've done for you in the past and what I will do for you in the future."

God had done so many things for Moses and the Israelites that His glory should never have been questioned. But at this time of intercession, Moses especially longed to know God even better. That is why he wanted the glory of God to be revealed to him in a special way.

As we consider that God's glory is revealed in His goodness, we have much to be thankful for, just as the Israelites did. God had done so many things for them out of His grace, in spite of the fact that they deserved exactly the opposite. This is also the way He has dealt with us. Because we are sinners, we all justly deserve condemnation. But because of His love and grace, the Lord Jesus Christ came in a human body and shed His blood on the cross to pay the penalty for our sin. "While we were yet sinners, Christ died for us" (Rom. 5:8). God cannot overlook sin—it has to be dealt with. This was true in Israel's case, and it is true in our case. Because of His character, God must always deal righteously and justly, and the penalty of sin had to be paid before anyone could enter heaven.

We are usually quick to categorize sin into gross sins and small sins, but as far as God is concerned, any sin is deserving of eternal condemnation. Of course, individual sins are the results of the sin nature which every person has. The Bible says, "As by one man sin entered into the world, and death by sin; and so death passed upon all men, for that all have sinned" (v. 12).

So sin has to be dealt with if any person is to be delivered from condemnation and enabled to enter the presence of God. The Old Testament sacrifices were a picture of *the* sacrifice—the Lord Jesus Christ—which would take away sin by paying its penalty. When Jesus Christ died on the cross, He paid the penalty for all sin—past, present and future.

No one benefits from Christ's finished work on the cross, however, unless he believes in Christ as his personal Saviour. A person has to change his mind about his own condition by admitting that he is a sinner. He also has to change his mind about Christ by admitting that Christ's shed blood paid the penalty for sin. When a person believes in Christ as Saviour, he indicates that he has changed his mind about these matters. Have you seen the awfulness of your sinful condition and trusted Jesus Christ as your personal Saviour? If so, you have received the forgiveness of sin, and you have eternal life. If not, you need to make this decision before it is eternally too late.

Commandments Given Again

Because Moses desired to see the glory of God in a special way, God placed Moses in a cleft of a rock and passed by him. But Moses was not allowed to look directly at God (see Ex. 33:22,23). Although it is difficult to understand all that took place when God revealed His glory to Moses at this time, it seemed to have satisfied Moses.

Then the grace of God was again manifested in that Moses was called back into His presence. We have no way of knowing how many times Moses ascended the mountain during this time of receiving the Law and interceding for the people. No doubt he went up and down the mountain several times as he communicated with God and then passed on this communication to the people.

The Lord told Moses, "Hew thee two tables of stone like unto the first: and I will write upon these tables the words that were in the first tables, which thou brakest. And be

ready in the morning, and come up in the morning unto
mount Sinai, and present thyself there to me in the top of
the mount" (34:1,2). Although the people had committed a
gross sin, God welcomed Moses again after he had interceded
for the people.

At this time God did not want any other person on the
mountain, and the animals were not to be in front of the
mountain. God said to Moses, "No man shall come up with
thee, neither let any man be seen throughout all the mount;
neither let the flocks nor herds feed before that mount"
(v. 3).

Moses did as the Lord told him: "He hewed two tables of
stone like unto the first; and Moses rose up early in the
morning, and went up unto mount Sinai, as the Lord had
commanded him, and took in his hand the two tables of
stone" (v. 4).

Israel, once again in full fellowship with God, was about
to receive the whole Law from the hand of God. God was
going to engrave another set of tablets containing the Ten
Commandments. But the whole Law included many more
commands. In fact, it is generally considered that, in all,
there were over 600 laws. This law system was entirely
binding on the people. The Bible says, "Whosoever shall keep
the whole law, and yet offend in one point, he is guilty of
all" (James 2:10). This verse refers not only to the Ten
Commandments but also to the other commands.

The Law given to Moses included moral, ceremonial and
civil regulations. In addition, God gave specific instructions
about the construction of the tabernacle and its use.

The moral law reflected the character of God; the
ceremonial law revealed God's justice and mercy; the civil law
dealt with relationships within the nation.

Moses had spent agonizing days—and maybe weeks—on
the mountain interceding for the sin of the people and had
won abundant mercies from God. Later, he saw the glory of
God in a special way. After that he was alone with God for
fellowship and to receive special revelation.

On the mountain, "the Lord said unto Moses, Write thou
these words: for after the tenor of these words I have made a
covenant with thee and with Israel. And he was there with
the Lord forty days and forty nights; he did neither eat

bread, nor drink water. And he [God] wrote upon the tables
the words of the covenant, the ten commandments" (Ex.
34:27,28).

Notice the miracle that occurred—Moses neither ate nor
drank for 40 days. This is humanly impossible and reveals
that God performed a miracle to sustain Moses during this
time.

Moses Reflects God's Glory

Moses was changed when he came down from the
mountain. Earlier, he had asked to see the glory of the Lord,
but when he came down from the mountain with the two
tablets of stone, he did not know "that the skin of his face
shone while he talked with him" (v. 29). Moses did not
realize that his face reflected the glory of God. This was
proof of the closeness between Moses and God, and it
revealed to those who saw him that he had truly been in the
presence of God's glory.

"When Aaron and all the children of Israel saw Moses,
behold, the skin of his face shone; and they were afraid to
come nigh him" (v. 30). Moses still did not realize the extent
to which his face reflected the glory of God. He was not
glorious in his own eyes, but he was in the eyes of others.

True Christian excellence is not conscious of its beauty.
Such glory is not seen by those who possess it; rather, it is
seen by those who behold the one who possesses it. Beware
of the person who talks about his own greatness. It is even
possible for a person to boast about his humility by
emphasizing his nothingness. Although he talks of his
nothingness, he may be inwardly proud of the way he
behaves and of the way God is using him.

Consider the contrasts between the two times Moses
descended from the mountain with the tablets of stone. The
first time, his face was distorted with anger because of the
Israelites' sin, and he threw down the tablets and shattered
them. The second time he descended with the tablets, his
face radiated the glory of God. Earlier he found the people
engaged in idolatry, but he later returned to a people
humbled by the mercies of God. The first time he descended
the mountain, Moses threw the tablets of stone to the

ground. The second time, he prepared to deposit them in the ark of the covenant, where they were to be kept.

The glory that was evidenced on Moses' face is a reminder of what the leaders in Jerusalem saw in the lives of Peter and John when they had been called before the Sanhedrin—the highest ruling court of the Jews. Peter and John had been preaching the gospel of the Lord Jesus Christ, and they were asked, "By what power, or by what name, have ye done this?" (Acts 4:7). Peter boldly answered the Sanhedrin and told the Jewish leaders, "Neither is there salvation in any other: for there is none other name under heaven given among men, whereby we must be saved" (v. 12). The Bible says, "When they saw the boldness of Peter and John, and perceived that they were unlearned and ignorant [untrained] men, they marvelled; and they took knowledge of them, that they had been with Jesus" (v. 13). Peter and John radiated the glory of the Lord Jesus Christ.

One cannot fellowship with the Lord Jesus Christ for very long without His glory being reflected in his life. Such a person does not need to wear a badge proclaiming his virtues or his victorious life—these will be evident to others.

When Aaron and the other Israelites saw the glory of God reflected in the face of Moses, "they were afraid to come nigh him" (Ex. 34:30). Perhaps they were afraid because God's reflected glory searched out their hearts and consciences, making them intensely aware that they could not, in themselves, meet even the smallest requirement of God's holiness. No doubt the reflected glory in Moses' face also emphasized their unworthiness—they knew they could not stand in God's presence as Moses had.

Can the glory of Christ be seen in those of us who have received Christ as Saviour? No one should ever attempt to minister God's message without first spending time in God's presence. God's glory must shine, not ours.

Every day before you go out to meet the world, spend some time with God by reading His Word and talking to Him in prayer. Spending time in His presence will bring the sunshine of heaven to your face, and others will observe this in you throughout the day.

Chapter 5
Israel Leaves Sinai

The Israelites had spent 11 months at Mount Sinai. They had come into the wilderness of Sinai in the third month after they were delivered from Egypt (Ex. 19:1,2). Numbers 10:11,12 records their leaving Sinai: "And it came to pass on the twentieth day of the second month, in the second year, that the cloud was taken up from off the tabernacle of the testimony. And the children of Israel took their journeys out of the wilderness of Sinai."

Wasted Time

The Israelites spent more time at Mount Sinai than should have been necessary because their sin had to be dealt with. They did receive the Law from God, along with specific instructions about the tabernacle and worship related to it. But most of the 11 months spent at Mount Sinai were apparently due to the sin of the people and the judgment and restitution that were necessary.

A principle seen throughout the Word of God is that time out of fellowship with the Lord is wasted time. Time spent in sin and in dealing with sin's results obviously shortens the time spent in effective fellowship and service.

Abraham is an example of one who lost time because of refusing to act immediately on the word of the Lord. He was instructed to leave his home and relatives and to go to a land that the Lord would show him (see Gen. 11:31; 12:1-3). As Abraham journeyed from his home in Ur of the Chaldees, however, he was with his relatives and remained with them when they reached Haran. Abraham wasted 15 years at

61

Haran, for it was not until his father died that he journeyed on to the land of Canaan as God had instructed.

Later, because of a famine in the land of Canaan, Abraham left the place of his altar and went to Egypt (12:10). Abraham had many heartaches in Egypt, but he finally returned to "Beth-el, unto the place where his tent had been at the beginning, between Beth-el and Hai; unto the place of the altar, which he had made there at the first: and there Abram called on the name of the Lord" (13:3,4). Here again, Abraham lost time while he was out of fellowship with God, for it was never intended that Abraham leave Canaan and go to Egypt.

Abraham's grandson Jacob also wasted time at Haran because he refused to follow God's program. Jacob spent 20 years at Haran with his father-in-law Laban. Even after Jacob returned to the land, he waited another ten years before he completely returned to the Lord and obeyed Him.

Later, the nation of Israel lost 38 years because of their refusal to follow God. It is important for every believer to realize that time spent out of fellowship with God is wasted time.

Perhaps you look back on wasted years and think that you have hardly any time left to offer the Lord. The important thing, however, is for the disobedient believer to confess his sins to the Lord and then to faithfully serve Him with whatever time he has left. No one knows how much time he has left to serve the Lord, so let us walk in obedience and honor Him in all that we do today.

Great Leadership

The evidence of divine leadership was first given to the Israelites in the form of the guiding cloud. The cloud first appeared after the Israelites were delivered from Egypt. "The Lord went before them by day in a pillar of a cloud, to lead them the way; and by night in a pillar of fire, to give them light; to go by day and night: he took not away the pillar of the cloud by day, nor the pillar of fire by night, from before the people" (Ex. 13:21,22).

As the Israelites prepared to leave Mount Sinai, the cloud was again the evidence of God's presence, although at this time it was associated with the tabernacle. "On the day that the tabernacle was reared up the cloud covered the tabernacle, namely, the tent of the testimony: and at even there was upon the tabernacle as it were the appearance of fire, until the morning. So it was alway: the cloud covered it by day, and the appearance of fire by night. And when the cloud was taken up from the tabernacle, then after that the children of Israel journeyed: and in the place where the cloud abode, there the children of Israel pitched their tents. At the commandment of the Lord the children of Israel journeyed, and at the commandment of the Lord they pitched: as long as the cloud abode upon the tabernacle they rested in their tents" (Num. 9:15-18).

So conscious were the Israelites of the guiding presence of God that "whether it were two days, or a month, or a year, that the cloud tarried upon the tabernacle, remaining thereon, the children of Israel abode in their tents, and journeyed not: but when it was taken up, they journeyed" (v. 22).

Any doubts as to who planned the strategy and led the Israelites were removed by the appearance of the cloud and the fire. The God of creation was the captain of the host—He called all the signals.

Later, the identity of the captain of the host was emphasized to Joshua. When Joshua was near Jericho, he saw a man with sword drawn and asked him, "Art thou for us, or for our adversaries?" (Josh. 5:13). The man answered, "Nay; but as captain of the host of the Lord am I now come. And Joshua fell on his face to the earth, and did worship, and said unto him, What saith my lord unto his servant? And the captain of the Lord's host said unto Joshua, Loose thy shoe from off thy foot; for the place whereon thou standest is holy. And Joshua did so" (vv. 14,15). It is important that we also know our captain.

God's provision of the cloud and the fire in association with the tabernacle was a clear, visible, undeniable and miraculous way of evidencing His divine presence with the Israelites. The cloud was miraculous in that it never dissipated nor did it move in the way that clouds commonly move. It often stayed in one place for an indefinite period of time (Num. 9:22). This cloud moved only when God wanted it to move, and even then it did not necessarily move in the direction of the wind. The Israelites could not initiate the moving of the cloud; it was God's prerogative.

We do not know exactly what the cloud looked like, but it was evident to the Israelites that God was with them if they remained in the presence of the cloud. At night the cloud took on the appearance of fire so that the camp had light even at night. As a result, the Israelites could move by night or by day.

Leading and Following

The cloud illustrates the principle of leading and following. It was God's responsibility to lead, and it was the people's responsibility to follow. The activity of the cloud was explicitly identified with the voice of God—"At the commandment of the Lord the children of Israel journeyed, and at the commandment of the Lord they pitched: as long as the cloud abode upon the tabernacle they rested in their tents" (Num. 9:18). The command at this time was given through Moses, but trumpets were later used to order the movements of the Israelites.

Israel's responsibility was to follow the signal of God. If the cloud moved, they were to move; if it did not move, they were not to move. Obedience to God is always the key to any spiritual success. If any believer wants to be successful in God's eyes, he must be obedient to God. God may lead the believer in ways he cannot understand, but the only responsibility of the Christian at such times is to follow Him.

Although the leadership of the Israelites was certainly divine, it also had human aspects. The Lord told Moses, "Make thee two trumpets of silver; of a whole piece shalt thou make them: that thou mayest use them for the calling of the assembly, and for the journeying of the camps. And when they shall blow with them, all the assembly shall assemble themselves to thee at the door of the tabernacle of the congregation. . . . And the sons of Aaron, the priests, shall blow with the trumpets; and they shall be to you for an ordinance for ever throughout your generations" (10:2,3,8).

As clear as the communications and revelations from God may be, He often chooses to use human leadership so that believers will not miss His directions through carelessness. Thus, the trumpets were blown by appointed leaders at certain times. Moses would consult with Aaron and his sons, and then the trumpets would be blown. If the people took their eyes off the cloud and closed their ears to the trumpets, they could not be led by God.

How thankful we should be today to have the unmistakable Word of God to give us leadership! Each believer should have the same attitude that the psalmist had as he prayed: "Search me, O God, and know my heart: try me, and know my thoughts: and see if there be any wicked way in me, and lead me in the way everlasting" (Ps. 139:23,24). Each of us who knows Jesus Christ as personal Saviour should desire to be led by God.

The Bible has much to say about the way believers are led. Before the Lord Jesus Christ ascended into heaven, He told the disciples, "Howbeit when he, the Spirit of truth, is come, he will guide you into all truth: for he shall not speak of himself; but whatsoever he shall hear, that shall he speak: and he will shew you things to come" (John 16:13). So the distinct ministry of the Holy Spirit is to guide believers into truth.

The leading of the Holy Spirit is not reserved for only some special group of believers; it is available to all believers. The Apostle Paul said, "For as many as are led by the Spirit of God, they are the sons of God" (Rom. 8:14). The Apostle Paul also told believers, "Walk in the Spirit, and ye shall not fulfil the lust of the flesh. . . . If we live in the Spirit, let us also walk in the Spirit" (Gal. 5:16,25).

As believers in Christ we need to recognize that God does not save us from condemnation and then just leave us here in this world to make it through our own self-efforts. Some Christians apparently attempt to live that way, but that is not the way God intended for us to live. A person cannot know what is best for himself; he must rely on the wisdom of God. Every believer needs to obey the injunctions of Proverbs 3:5-7: "Trust in the Lord with all thine heart; and lean not unto thine own understanding. In all thy ways acknowledge him, and he shall direct thy paths. Be not wise in thine own eyes: fear the Lord, and depart from evil."

I personally receive much help in finding God's leadership by meditating on Psalm 25. Psalm 119 is also a great encouragement—it points to the Word of God as the heavenly means of leadership.

Israel's First Move

The Bible says, "It came to pass on the twentieth day of the second month, in the second year, that the cloud was taken up from off the tabernacle of the testimony. And the children of Israel took their journeys out of the wilderness of Sinai; and the cloud rested in the wilderness of Paran" (Num. 10:11,12).

The tabernacle was in the center of the camp, so the cloud was visible to all. As soon as the cloud lifted, the Israelites knew they were to move. "They departed from the mount of the Lord three days' journey: and the ark of the covenant of the Lord went before them in the three days' journey, to search out a resting place for them. And the cloud of the Lord was upon them by day, when they went out of the camp" (vv. 33,34).

The 11 months at Sinai had brought about many changes in the life of Israel. The people had arrived at Sinai a fugitive and unorganized people; they left a well-organized nation, molded into a commonwealth of 12 tribes. All was beautifully ordered. At this time God used the special training Moses had received in Egypt. "Moses was learned in all the wisdom of the Egyptians, and was mighty in words and in deeds" (Acts 7:22).

Moses had spent the first 40 years of his life being trained in the courts of Pharaoh as a possible successor to Pharaoh. As such, Moses was trained in organization and was the general of the Egyptian army. He learned all that would be necessary to lead the greatest nation on earth at that time. Moses used all the knowledge he had accumulated in leading the Israelites. It was not, however, the unaided genius of Moses that God used. God leads through minds competent to receive and transmit His teaching. In Moses' case, his mental abilities were used to transmit to Israel an order of organization that was second to none. What Moses had learned in the world was translated into use for the glory of God.

The Israelites left Sinai as a mighty nation in battle array. They had been furnished with a code of laws, including sanitary regulations, which have been a model for civilized peoples of the world. They had also been provided with a system of sacrifices that continued for centuries. These sacrifices prophetically pointed to the priesthood of the Lord Jesus Christ for believers.

The tabernacle was completed and furnished, providing a special place to meet God. The cloud hovered over the tabernacle as an evidence that God's presence was with the people. When the people saw the cloud lifting and heard the blasting of the trumpets, they moved as they had been instructed. The tribe of Judah went first, and then Issachar, Zebulun and the other tribes followed in order. What a beautiful array it must have been to see three million people moving in such orderliness!

Even though the presence of God was clearly evident to the people, they complained. "And when the people complained, it displeased the Lord: and the Lord heard it; and his anger was kindled; and the fire of the Lord burnt among them, and consumed them that were in the uttermost parts of the camp" (Num. 11:1). God had been dealing with the Israelites on the basis of pure grace, but now He began to deal with them on the basis of the Law. Their murmuring was punishable, so God sent fire to destroy them.

But Moses stood in the gap again: "The people cried unto Moses; and when Moses prayed unto the Lord, the fire was quenched" (v. 2). The psalmist wrote: "Therefore he said that he would destroy them, had not Moses his chosen stood before him in the breach, to turn away his wrath, lest he should destroy them" (Ps. 106:23). Moses was faithful in interceding for his people.

Although Moses had wonderful opportunities for self-advancement, never was his selflessness more clearly evident than when he boldly and persistently prayed to God for Israel. In so doing, Moses averted God's judgments on the often-apostate nation.

The Mixed Multitude

The Scriptures are totally honest when giving information about a person. For instance, many great moments of Moses' life are revealed, but the Scriptures also tell of his weaker moments. One such occasion involved the mixed multitude that came with the Israelites out of Egypt.

The mixed multitude was probably a group of Gentiles who left Egypt with the Israelites. They are first mentioned in Exodus 12:38. After the Israelites had left Mount Sinai, "the mixt multitude that was among them fell a lusting: and the children of Israel also wept again, and said, Who shall give us flesh to eat? We remember the fish, which we did eat in Egypt freely; the cucumbers, and the melons, and the leeks, and the onions, and the garlick: but now our soul is dried away: there is nothing at all, beside this manna, before our eyes" (Num. 11:4-6).

Although the complaining was started by the mixed multitude, the Israelites were also guilty of complaining. This indicates how infectious a complaining attitude can be. Because every person has a sin nature, it does not take long even for believers to become disheartened and to develop an attitude of complaining against the goodness of God. After salvation, Christians too often remember what they enjoyed in the world and occasionally long for the pleasures of sin. When this happens, the believer is guilty of leaving his first love.

The Church of Ephesus was guilty of this, and Christ told it, "Remember therefore from whence thou art fallen, and repent, and do the first works; or else I will come unto thee quickly, and will remove thy candlestick out of his place, except thou repent" (Rev. 2:5). Romans 8:5-8 emphasizes that the believer is to seek the things of the Spirit, not the things of the flesh. Verse 7 reveals that the carnal, or fleshly, mind is "enmity against God." Therefore, those who live to fulfill the desires of the flesh cannot please God.

Christians who have not grown spiritually as they should, through the reading of God's Word and applying it to daily life, find it easy to murmur as the Israelites did. Only a small minority may begin the complaining, but the Christian who is not mature is also susceptible. Just as the bark of one dog can start a whole group of dogs barking, one complaining believer can affect an entire group.

Many pastors have had their hearts broken, and church work has been greatly hampered by a few disgruntled people who influence the entire church. Every church group seems to have a few people who find it easy to complain about anything. Unless the other believers are mature, they will soon follow the pattern of the murmuring, weak believer.

The Israelites may have given no thought to being dissatisfied with the manna that had been miraculously provided for them. But when they heard the complaint of the mixed multitude, they also decided they were tired of eating the same food day after day.

The mixed multitude is a reminder of those who are not believers. The New Testament refers to an unbeliever as a "natural" man, and I Corinthians 2:14 says, "The natural man receiveth not the things of the Spirit of God: for they are foolishness unto him: neither can he know them, because they are spiritually discerned."

Believers who are caught up in a worldly spirit or attitude are referred to as carnal. First Corinthians 3:1,2 says, "And I, brethren, could not speak unto you as unto spiritual, but as unto carnal, even as unto babes in Christ. I have fed you with milk, and not with meat: for hitherto ye were not able to bear it, neither yet now are ye able." These carnal, or fleshly, believers are not able to concentrate on the deep things of God because they are still thinking about fulfilling the desires of the flesh. They find it easy to complain if they are not satisfied, and their complaints can have a deadening effect on others.

God Deals With the Complaints

Notice how God dealt with the murmuring of the mixed multitude. God told Moses, "Say thou unto the people, Sanctify yourselves against to morrow, and ye shall eat flesh: for ye have wept in the ears of the Lord, saying, Who shall give us flesh to eat? For it was well with us in Egypt: therefore the Lord will give you flesh, and ye shall eat" (Num. 11:18). As if this promise were not enough, God added: "Ye shall not eat one day, nor two days, nor five days, neither ten days, nor twenty days; but even a whole month, until it come out at your nostrils, and it be loathsome unto you: because that ye have despised the Lord which is among you, and have wept before him, saying, Why came we forth out of Egypt?" (vv. 19,20).

Notice Moses' response to what God said. At this point Moses revealed that he had moved from being a great intercessor to being a doubter. God promised to supply meat for an entire month, but Moses said, "The people, among whom I am, are six hundred thousand footmen; and thou hast said, I will give them flesh, that they may eat a whole month. Shall the flocks and the herds be slain for them, to suffice them? Or shall all the fish of the sea be gathered together for them, to suffice them?" (vv. 21,22).

God rebuked Moses for his doubt, but He rebuked him gently: "Is the Lord's hand waxed short? Thou shalt see now whether my word shall come to pass unto thee or not" (v. 23). Moses had doubts about God's ability to supply meat for an entire month. Possibly, his doubts were aggravated by his great weariness and by the heavy burden of leading the people. Satan has a way of attacking us when we are down. Remember Amalek? He came when the Israelites were tired and weak; he struck from behind, surprising Israel (see Ex. 17:8-16).

God remained faithful to His promise; He supplied meat for a month just as He said He would. "There went forth a wind from the Lord, and brought quails from the sea, and let them fall by the camp, as it were a day's journey on this side, and as it were a day's journey on the other side, round about the camp, and as it were two cubits high upon the face of the earth" (Num. 11:31). The expression "two cubits high upon the face of the earth" has been variously interpreted. At first glance it seems that the quail were piled that high on the earth. But a legitimate interpretation of the expression is that God caused the quail to fly two cubits, or about three feet, above the ground so the Israelites could catch them.

The people gathered all they could and were beginning to enjoy the feast they had so longed for, but "while the flesh was yet between their teeth, ere [before] it was chewed, the wrath of the Lord was kindled against the people, and the Lord smote the people with a very great plague" (v. 33).

In commenting about the Israelites and this incident, the psalmist said, "They soon forgat his works; they waited not for his counsel: but lusted exceedingly in the wilderness, and tempted God in the desert. And he gave them their request; but sent leanness into their soul" (Ps. 106:13-15).

God may answer believers today in the same way. If we are guilty of complaining and continue to ask God for things just to satisfy our own fleshly desires, He may grant our request, but the result will be spiritual leanness.

Are you out of fellowship with the Lord? Are you seeking to be satisfied with things rather than with the Person of Christ? If so, learn from the example of the Israelites, confess your sin and be restored to fellowship. You will then discover that the Word of God is more precious than you ever thought possible. But when unconfessed sin is in your life, the Word of God becomes tiresome, and one is tempted to complain about the same spiritual diet day after day. But the believer who realizes the awfulness of sin will be so appreciative of God's grace and forgiveness that the Word of God will be a thrill to his heart. As Jeremiah said, "Thy words were found, and I did eat them; and thy word was unto me the joy and rejoicing of mine heart: for I am called by thy name, O Lord God of hosts" (Jer. 15:16).

Chapter 6

Moses Personally Attacked

Crises do not produce heroes, nor do they make cowards. However, when a person is exposed to extraordinary circumstances, strengths and weaknesses come to light that even he did not know he had. As a storm beats against an oak tree, it may reveal the strength of the tree and its ability to stand, or it may reveal hidden decay as the tree collapses under the storm.

Few men can be in a position of influence and power and not be adversely affected. Many can stand under reproof and rebuke and be benefited, but human nature is such that the glamour of position and power becomes a snare.

Someone has said, "We are not what we are because of what we do; we do what we do because of what we are." Another way to put it is that "character determines the deed" or "the deed only reveals the character."

Moses was severely tested in his high position of power. There were three specific attacks, or severe tests, that involved three people: himself, Miriam and Korah.

Discouragement Attacks Moses

Moses himself was involved in the sin of discouragement. Moses was a tried servant, but he was also a tired one, and he became guilty of charging God with unfairness. When the people grumbled because they had only manna to eat, "Moses heard the people weep throughout their families, every man in the door of his tent: and the anger of the Lord was kindled greatly; Moses also was displeased" (Num. 11:10).

In his displeasure Moses said to the Lord, "Wherefore hast thou afflicted thy servant? And wherefore have I not found favour in thy sight, that thou layest the burden of all this people upon me? Have I conceived all this people? Have I begotten them, that thou shouldest say unto me, Carry them in thy bosom, as a nursing father beareth the sucking child, unto the land which thou swarest unto their fathers? Whence should I have flesh to give unto all this people? For they weep unto me, saying, Give us flesh, that we may eat. I am not able to bear all this people alone, because it is too heavy for me. And if thou deal thus with me, kill me, I pray thee, out of hand, if I have found favour in thy sight; and let me not see my wretchedness" (vv. 11-15).

Moses had finally become so discouraged he could not take it any longer, so he complained to God. His complaining was different, however, than the complaining of the people. They had taken out their complaints on him, but he did not respond by attacking them; instead, he went to God and poured out his heart to Him. What a lesson this is for every believer! Each one needs to take his burdens to the Lord in prayer. God understood what Moses was going through. As the psalmist said, God "knoweth our frame; he remembereth that we are dust" (Ps. 103:14).

Caught in a weak moment, Moses lost sight of the sovereignty of God and began to feel sorry for himself. This did not happen very often in Moses' life, but it shows how human Moses was. Self-pity is destructive and reflects itself both in a person's moral life and in his spiritual life. It is common for people, because of their weak sin natures, to fall prey to the attacks of Satan at such a time. Only Jesus Christ, who was the God-Man, was always able to resist the attacks of Satan.

Moses was particularly discouraged because he had just interceded for the people, asking that they be spared from further judgment by God. Now they were murmuring again. God was providing manna miraculously, and yet the people complained about this provision.

This reveals that even 15 months after they had left Egypt, the people still had their hearts fixed on Egypt. Moses was physically exhausted, and then his patience became exhausted. He was vulnerable to Satan's attack.

Elijah had a similar experience. He had been on Mount Carmel and had experienced tremendous victory for the Lord (see I Kings 18). Because of Elijah's strong stand for the Lord, he became responsible for destroying 850 false prophets. After this he ran "before Ahab to the entrance of Jezreel" (v. 46). Then, when Elijah heard that Jezebel planned to do to him what he had done to the false prophets, "he arose, and went for his life, and came to Beer-sheba" (19:3). Elijah left his servant at Beersheba and then "went a day's journey into the wilderness, and came and sat down under a juniper tree: and he requested for himself that he might die; and said, It is enough; now, O Lord, take away my life; for I am not better than my fathers" (v. 4). Elijah was exhausted physically, which made him vulnerable to Satan's attacks.

When Moses was physically exhausted, he was also susceptible to Satan's attack of discouragement. He was so distraught that he wanted to die if the Lord did not change the situation with the people. In his discouragement Moses apparently felt that God had heaped all the burdens on him and that there was no divine help when it was really needed.

God's Reaction to Moses' Discouragement

Because the Lord understood all that Moses was going through, He did not rebuke him. Instead, the Lord told Moses, "Gather unto me seventy men of the elders of Israel, whom thou knowest to be the elders of the people, and officers over them; and bring them unto the tabernacle of the congregation, that they may stand there with thee. And I will come down and talk with thee there" (Num. 11:16,17).

Even though God would be speaking specifically with Moses, the 70 elders would hear what God had to say to him. The Lord told Moses what He planned to do: "I will take of the spirit which is upon thee, and will put it upon them; and they shall bear the burden of the people with thee, that thou bear it not thyself alone" (v. 17).

Moses did as he was instructed. He "went out, and told the people the words of the Lord, and gathered the seventy men of the elders of the people, and set them round about the tabernacle. And the Lord came down in a cloud, and spake unto him, and took of the spirit that was upon him, and gave it unto the seventy elders: and it came to pass, that, when the spirit rested upon them, they prophesied, and did not cease" (vv. 24,25).

God alleviated Moses' aloneness in his responsibility by providing 70 others to share the load. It is commonly thought that the Spirit which was on Moses was divided among the 70 elders. I cannot agree with this position, however, because it is impossible to diminish the Spirit of God. One does not draw off portions of the Holy Spirit as he draws off water from a well. Rather, it seems more accurate to understand verse 25 as teaching that the same Spirit who was on Moses was also given to the 70 elders. Thus, the Spirit who was on Moses was not diminished, but He also rested on the 70 for this special task.

The entire Spirit of God filled, or controlled, each man completely for the task at hand. Just as a flame of fire reaches out to engulf other objects, the Holy Spirit's resting on Moses was extended to the others so that the entire group could be effective for the Lord. There were then 71 lights instead of just one.

Just as one could use the fire from one candle to light 70 others, the Holy Spirit in His full essence was on the 70 elders without being diminished in Moses' life. If God chose to create new stars, He would not have to diminish the light from the sun to give brilliance to the stars. Instead, God would use the same force operable in the sun to give light to the stars.

Concerning the Holy Spirit, it is important to observe the difference between His relationship with believers in the Old Testament and believers in the New Testament. During Old Testament times, the Holy Spirit came on whomever God chose and rested on them or worked through them to accomplish a specific task as God willed and purposed. When the task was accomplished, the Holy Spirit apparently then left that person. This is why David prayed, "Do not take Thy Holy Spirit from me" (Ps. 51:11, NASB).

During New Testament times, however, the Holy Spirit indwelt every believer, as He does today. Romans 8:9 says, "If anyone does not have the Spirit of Christ, he does not belong to Him" (NASB). The fact that every believer's body is inhabited by the Holy Spirit is also seen in I Corinthians 6:19: "Do you not know that your body is a temple of the Holy Spirit who is in you, whom you have from God, and that you are not your own?" (NASB).

Moses' Character Revealed

When God distributed the Spirit that was on Moses to the 70 elders, they began to prophesy (Num. 11:25). This created a situation that revealed the noble character of Moses. When two men were discovered continuing in their prophesying and it was not understood why, a young man ran to tell Moses. Joshua, a special servant to Moses, said, "My lord Moses, forbid them" (v. 28). But notice the beautiful response of Moses: "Enviest thou for my sake? Would God that all the Lord's people were prophets, and that the Lord would put his spirit upon them!" (v. 29).

Moses harbored no jealousy at all. Joshua was jealous for his master, but he did not need to be. However, even this was an indication of Joshua's total loyalty to Moses. He did not want others usurping the authority that belonged only to Moses. Joshua did not want Moses' prestige diminished in any way.

But envy and jealousy found no lodging in Moses' generous nature. He could safely leave such matters in the hands of God, because he had not chosen his own responsibility of leadership—that was God's doing. This is a reminder of something the Lord Jesus said which applies to present-day believers: "Ye have not chosen me, but I have chosen you, and ordained you, that ye should go and bring forth fruit, and that your fruit should remain: that whatsoever ye shall ask of the Father in my name, he may give it you" (John 15:16).

Moses was in touch with God, and a spiritual leader in touch with God does not need to be concerned about his prestige or prerogatives—he can leave those in God's hands.

Psalm 37:5,6 reveals what the believer needs to do: "Commit your way to the Lord, trust also in Him, and He will do it. And He will bring forth your righteousness as the light, and your judgment as the noonday" (NASB). God will take care of the believer and will eventually vindicate him just as surely as the sun shines at noonday.

Moses' reaction revealed a spirit of greatness. He rejoiced when others shared honor with him. When a person's desires are eagerly and intently concentrated on seeing God's will done, the glory of that light extinguishes the fire of self-ambition. A true and faithful servant is willing to be anything—or nothing—if only the divine purpose of God is accomplished.

Miriam and Aaron Attack Moses

Because Moses was used so distinctly by God in leading Israel, it was not unusual for others to be jealous of his leadership position. Numbers 12:1 says, "Miriam and Aaron spake against Moses because of the Ethiopian woman whom he had married: for he had married an Ethiopian woman."

Miriam and Aaron were Moses' older sister and brother. But even they took issue with Moses' leadership, although at first their complaints concerned his wife. Numbers 12 does not specifically say what Miriam and Aaron found objectionable about Moses' wife, but jealousy must have been the main problem.

Moses' wife had just recently joined him at Mount Sinai. Moses had married when he was in the wilderness in the "school" of God. When he returned to Egypt to deliver Israel, however, he went alone. So Moses was without his wife for over a year. Then his father-in-law brought her to him at Mount Sinai.

During the time Moses was without his wife, it is likely that Miriam took care of the housekeeping duties and looked after Moses' welfare. But with the return of Moses' wife, Miriam was put in second place, and she revolted by attacking Moses' leadership.

It is understandable that Miriam was jealous, because she had had a distinctive part in Moses' life. She had watched over him when he was a baby and was hidden among the reeds on the River Nile (see Ex. 2:3,4). Miriam had actively supported Moses when he led the Israelites out of Egypt and had even led the women in a song of praise after their escape (see 15:20,21).

But then Miriam and Aaron complained about Moses' wife, perhaps because they were excluded from that inner family circle. Miriam and Aaron may have gossiped together about Moses' wife. Perhaps Miriam was the instigator of the gossip, but Aaron joined her in it—the Bible indicates that both were involved in this complaining against Moses. Both Miriam and Aaron were older than Moses, and perhaps it was difficult for them to bow to the leadership of their younger brother.

This jealousy took its usual hypocritical turn. Miriam and Aaron did not talk to Moses about his wife; instead, they complained about his authority. How easy it is to disguise jealousy beneath a cloak of zeal for the law of God or to think of oneself as pure while rebuking somebody else's faults. Real jealousy originates from power hunger, and it usually breaks out in faultfinding, just as it did in this case.

Miriam and Aaron said, "Hath the Lord indeed spoken only by Moses? Hath he not spoken also by us?" (Num. 12:2). But even though they did not realize the seriousness of the charge, the Bible says, "And the Lord heard it" (v. 2).

If only believers would always remember that the Lord is listening in on their conversations, which means He hears all of their accusations. If they would keep this in mind, many gossiping tongues would be silenced. God is listening to every word you say to someone about another person.

The psalmist said, "The Lord knoweth the thoughts of man, that they are vanity" (Ps. 94:11). There are no thoughts a person has that the Lord does not know. The psalmist also said, "Search me, O God, and know my heart: try me, and know my thoughts: and see if there be any wicked way in me, and lead me in the way everlasting" (139:23,24).

Someone has said, "When we think we are judging another, God is often judging our own state." It is a trait of the flesh when aroused to jealousy to cut others down to fit one's own pattern.

Because we all have a sin nature, we tend to think that we can exalt ourselves by disparaging others. This is especially true in the political world. One person running for office endeavors to make himself look the most qualified for the position by putting down the other candidates. Perhaps

Miriam and Aaron thought the only way to add to their prestige was to take away from Moses' prestige.

Moses' Meekness

At this point the Bible says, "(Now the man Moses was very meek, above all the men which were upon the face of the earth)" (Num. 12:3). This was God's estimate of Moses. When Miriam and Aaron made their charges, Moses did not answer a word—he reflected the character of God.

Believers today have the Holy Spirit living within them, and they manifest the fruit of the Spirit as they submit to Him (see Gal. 5:22,23).

The Apostle Peter told believers, "For even hereunto were ye called: because Christ also suffered for us, leaving us an example, that ye should follow his steps: who did no sin, neither was guile found in his mouth: who, when he was reviled, reviled not again; when he suffered, he threatened not; but committed himself to him that judgeth righteously" (I Pet. 2:21-23).

Our ability to respond in this way is made possible by the indwelling Christ. That Christ indwells believers is evident from Colossians 1:27: "Christ in you, the hope of glory." Because Christ was in him, the Apostle Paul went on to say in verse 29, "For this purpose also I labor, striving according to His power, which mightily works within me" (NASB).

The Bible's reference to Moses' being "very meek" (Num. 12:3) does not mean that he was weak. Meekness is not weakness. The weak return blow for blow and blurt out their wrath because they are unable to control their passion. Meekness, on the other hand, does not defend itself. Only a strong person can remain quiet when he is provoked and even turn the provocation into an intense love for the person accusing him. No wonder Jesus said, "Blessed are the meek: for they shall inherit the earth" (Matt. 5:5).

Because of Moses' meekness, he did not get angry with Miriam and Aaron, which caused God to have great praise for him. Meekness is really the result of true humility. Humility refers to one's attitude, especially a person's attitude toward God. Meekness is the outward manifestation to others of the inner relationship and attitude toward God.

A meek person is under control; in particular, he is under the control of God, for only God can give a person the mastery of himself when he is provoked.

When the Bible refers to being "filled with the Spirit" (Eph. 5:18), it refers to a person's being under the control of the Holy Spirit. The Holy Spirit forms the life and attitudes of Christ in the believer. When the believer is under the control of the Holy Spirit, he will react toward his enemies the same way Christ reacted toward His.

Meekness indicates that there is no sense of self-assertion. The meek person is not vindictive nor is he quick to defend himself. Moses relied on the Lord to vindicate him when he was charged by Miriam and Aaron. Thus, in Moses we see a combination of great moral and spiritual strength as well as genuine humility. All of these are marks of a man of God. The person who walks in right relationship with God does not need to vindicate himself. The believer is assured in Psalm 37:6 that God "will bring forth your righteousness as the light, and your judgment as the noonday" (NASB).

Question for Believers

Each believer needs to answer a searching question: Are my eyes fixed on the single purpose of glorifying God? If so, the fires of self-ambition will be extinguished. When a believer desires to glorify God above all else, he will be willing to do anything and to be anything so that the purpose of God can be accomplished.

The Apostle Paul gave believers admonitions about living for the glory of God. Paul said, "Let no one seek his own good, but that of his neighbor. . . . Whether, then, you eat or drink or whatever you do, do all to the glory of God" (I Cor. 10:24,31, NASB). Concerning himself, Paul said, "Just as I also please all men in all things, not seeking my own profit, but the profit of the many, that they may be saved" (v. 33, NASB).

It is good for a believer to ask himself if he is as concerned about seeing God's working through others as he is about God's working through himself. The sin nature causes a person to want to be on center stage. We are all like this, so we must come to grips with this tendency. We become competitive in the Christian life and find it difficult to pray for Christians who are not part of our church or our work.

But in the Body of Christ there should be no competing with each other. We are members of the same body (I Cor. 12:12,13), and when one member suffers, we should all suffer with him. When one member is honored, we should all rejoice (v. 26).

We need to spend time in the Word and be alone with God until we are more concerned about His honor than our own. We do not have to worry about competition from other believers; our concern is only to glorify the Lord in all that we do. When a Christian is more concerned about God's honor than about his own, God will take care of his worries about competition from fellow believers. Granted, it is much easier to say this than to really live it, but we must come to grips with this problem if we are going to have victory in our Christian lives. We must be aware of the indwelling Christ and rely on Him to give us victory in these areas.

Since Jesus Christ lives within the believer, the characteristics of Christ will be expressed through the believer when self is out of the way. And what are the characteristics of Christ? Notice what kind of an attitude the Lord Jesus Christ had: "Have this attitude in yourselves which was also in Christ Jesus, who, although He existed in the form of God, did not regard equality with God a thing to be grasped, but emptied Himself, taking the form of a bondservant, and being made in the likeness of men. And being found in appearance as a man, He humbled Himself by becoming obedient to the point of death, even death on a cross" (Phil. 2:5-8, NASB).

A meek and quiet spirit are very valuable in the sight of God, but how does the believer obtain such a spirit? First, claim the meekness of Christ. There was no guile, or deceit, in Jesus Christ, and He did not retaliate against His enemies (see I Pet. 2:21-23). Ask Christ to produce this kind of meekness in you. The Lord Jesus said, "Take my yoke upon you, and learn of me; for I am meek and lowly in heart: and ye shall find rest unto your souls" (Matt. 11:29). In any moment of provocation, turn at once to the Lord Jesus Christ, and claim His meekness.

Second, cultivate the habit of silence. The psalmist said, "What time I am afraid, I will trust in thee" (Ps. 56:3). Isaiah 30:15 tells the believer, "In quietness and in confidence shall be your strength." James 1:19 admonishes, "Let every man be swift to hear, slow to speak, slow to wrath."

Third, consider the harm done to the aggressors. One cannot say unkind and bitter words about others without hurting himself more than others.

Fourth, let God vindicate your cause. Moses trusted God to vindicate him, so he did not try to defend himself. God heard the unjust accusations, and a righteous God would not leave such injustice without correction. Commit yourself to the Lord, and He who judges righteously will vindicate you (see Ps. 37:5,6). The believer can safely leave his case with the Lord, knowing that God will bring to pass what is right and necessary.

God's Response to Miriam and Aaron

Even though Moses did not respond to the charges of Miriam and Aaron, "the Lord spake suddenly unto Moses, and unto Aaron, and unto Miriam, Come out ye three unto the tabernacle of the congregation" (Num. 12:4). Thus we see that the Lord took immediate action when accusations were made against the leader He had chosen. The Lord had heard the accusations made by Miriam and Aaron, and He spoke audibly to them and commanded that they come to the tabernacle.

At the tabernacle, "the Lord came down in the pillar of the cloud, and stood in the door of the tabernacle, and called Aaron and Miriam: and they both came forth. And he said, Hear now my words: If there be a prophet among you, I the Lord will make myself known unto him in a vision, and will speak unto him in a dream. My servant Moses is not so, who is faithful in all mine house. With him will I speak mouth to mouth, even apparently, and not in dark speeches; and the similitude of the Lord shall he behold: wherefore then were ye not afraid to speak against my servant Moses?" (vv. 5-8).

At least three specific elements in this passage need special attention. First, God made it clear to Miriam and Aaron that He revealed Himself to prophets by visions and dreams (v. 6). Although this was God's normal way of revealing Himself to mankind, He made it clear to Miriam and Aaron that this was not the way He revealed Himself to Moses.

Second, God chose to reveal Himself to Moses in a most intimate way—"mouth to mouth, even apparently, and not in dark speeches; and the similitude of the Lord shall he behold" (v. 8).

Third, the Lord asked Miriam and Aaron, "Wherefore then were ye not afraid to speak against my servant Moses?" (v. 8).

Miriam and Aaron were guilty before God because of their accusations of Moses. The Bible says, "The anger of the Lord was kindled against them; and he departed" (v. 9).

Notice the consequences of the accusations made by Miriam and Aaron: "Miriam became leprous, white as snow" (v. 10). When Aaron saw what had happened to Miriam, he said to Moses, "I beseech thee, lay not the sin upon us, wherein we have done foolishly, and wherein we have sinned" (v. 11). This admission by Aaron was a confession of his sin. Even though I John 1:9 had not yet been written, the truth it states was as applicable in Aaron's time as in ours: "If we confess our sins, he is faithful and just to forgive us our sins, and to cleanse us from all unrighteousness."

Because Aaron confessed his sin by admitting it, he was forgiven by God, and judgment did not fall on him. However, Miriam experienced judgment, indicating she was unwilling at that time to admit her sin.

Aaron pleaded for his sister in the condition that had been brought on her. Aaron said to Moses, "Let her not be as one dead, of whom the flesh is half consumed when he cometh out of his mother's womb" (Num. 12:12). Miriam's flesh was decomposing as a result of the leprosy, and Aaron was desperately pleading that his older sister not be like a stillborn child that comes into the world with decomposed flesh.

Moses Intercedes for Miriam

In response to Aaron's plea, Moses "cried unto the Lord, saying, Heal her now, O God, I beseech thee" (Num. 12:13).

Moses revealed his godlike character by pleading for Miriam instead of rebuking her in anger. He interceded for his older sister and appealed to God on the basis of His name *El*, which is related to *Elohim*, the name used in reference to His creative work. Moses appealed for an act that only the God of creation could accomplish—making living flesh from dead flesh.

Moses' godlike character is seen in that he appealed for Miriam's healing, even though he was the one being directly attacked by her accusations.

The way a believer responds to others depends on his own relationship to the Lord. The New Testament tells believers, "Woe unto you, when all men shall speak well of you! For so did their fathers to the false prophets. But I say unto you which hear, Love your enemies, do good to them which hate you, bless them that curse you, and pray for them which despitefully use you" (Luke 6:26-28).

Notice God's response to Moses' intercessory prayer for Miriam: "The Lord said unto Moses, If her father had but spit in her face, should she not be ashamed seven days? Let her be shut out from the camp seven days, and after that let her be received in again" (Num. 12:14).

Miriam was kept outside the camp for seven days while the Israelites waited before they moved on (v. 15). The Lord responded in grace to the intercessory prayer of Moses but only after justice was done. Speaking out against the servant that God had chosen to lead the Israelites was a great sin, and God revealed to the people how serious He considered it to be.

The awfulness and hideousness of Miriam's sin was exposed. She was not restored to the camp until she had paid for the sin of haughtiness and envy by being shut outside the camp in humiliation for seven days. She did not atone for her sin—no person can do that—but she did experience the consequences of her sin. She also experienced the timeless truth that a person reaps whatever he sows (Gal. 6:7).

All Israel knew about her sin and its punishment because they were delayed in their journey for seven days. Think of it—three million people had to wait for one person! She may have committed her sin privately, but she was exposed to public shame. It is good to remember that no sin is really private. What any individual does has an effect on others.

It is also important to remember that any consequences the believer suffers for his sin cannot be compared to what Christ suffered for the sin of the world. The Bible says, "Wherefore Jesus also, that he might sanctify the people with his own blood, suffered without the gate" (Heb. 13:12). Because of what the Lord Jesus Christ did for us, let all of us who know Him as Saviour do what the following verse exhorts: "Let us go forth therefore unto him without the camp, bearing his reproach" (v. 13).

Korah Attacks Moses

Moses had undergone the attack of Satan through personal discouragement and the attack by Miriam concerning his authority. Now he was about to undergo the most subtle of all attacks. Note how the attacks became progressively more severe. As we grow in our knowledge of God, He often tests us more severely to develop a stronger character. But we should always remember I Corinthians 10:13: "No temptation has overtaken you but such as is common to man; and God is faithful, who will not allow you to be tempted beyond what you are able, but with the temptation will provide the way of escape also, that you may be able to endure it" (NASB).

The rebellion of Korah occurred several years after Miriam and Aaron allowed their jealousy to erupt into accusations against Moses. Korah's rebellion is described in Numbers 16. Following him in his rebellion were 250 princes described as "men of renown" (v. 2). Of course, they were not renowned before God but before men. These princes were highly respected leaders among the Israelites.

Korah and these princes "gathered themselves together against Moses and against Aaron, and said unto them, Ye take too much upon you, seeing all the congregation are holy, every one of them, and the Lord is among them: wherefore then lift ye up yourselves above the congregation of the Lord?" (v. 3). This accusation and attack on Moses was similar to the previous attack by Miriam and Aaron but seemed much more severe. Both cases involved jealousy of the leadership of another, although at this time Aaron was accused along with Moses of lording it over the people.

Korah and his followers indicated that the leadership of Moses and Aaron was no longer needed. Korah and his followers pointed out, "All the congregation are holy, every one of them, and the Lord is among them" (v. 3). Korah and his men were pointing out that any one of the Israelites was just as qualified as Moses and Aaron to lead the people. In this charge they specifically ignored God's prerogative of choice, for He had distinctly chosen Moses and Aaron to lead the people.

Korah and his followers also implied that they were qualified to do the priestly tasks when they asked Moses and Aaron, "Wherefore then lift ye up yourselves above the congregation of the Lord?" (v. 3). This question really leveled an accusation at God, because He had distinctly put Moses and Aaron into the positions they held. Moses had been reluctant to accept God's call, but finally God persuaded him to obey. It must have hurt Moses deeply to have Korah and his followers charge him with placing himself above the others.

Any suggestion that every person was qualified to be a priest was seriously out of line. God guarded the priesthood closely—anyone who intruded into the priestly office was put to death. This indicates how calloused Korah and his followers had become. They were even thinking of taking upon themselves the priestly activities.

Korah and the 250 princes also charged Moses with not bringing them into the land as he had promised. They asked Moses, "Is it a small thing that thou hast brought us up out of a land that floweth with milk and honey, to kill us in the wilderness, except thou make thyself altogether a prince over us? Moreover thou hast not brought us into a land that floweth with milk and honey, or given us inheritance of fields and vineyards: wilt thou put out the eyes of these men?" (vv. 13,14).

What an accusation! It was not Moses' responsibility to bring the Israelites into the land; it was God's responsibility. The people were the ones causing the delay.

Moses' Response to Korah

Notice how Moses responded to the various charges. First, "he fell upon his face" (Num. 16:4). This is a reference to the way Moses prostrated himself before God. Then he responded by telling Korah and his followers: "Even to morrow the Lord will shew who are his, and who is holy; and will cause him to come near unto him" (v. 5).

Later, Moses spoke to the other Israelites concerning Korah and his followers: "Hereby ye shall know that the Lord hath sent me to do all these works; for I have not done them of mine own mind. If these men die the common death of all men, or if they be visited after the visitation of all men, then the Lord hath not sent me. But if the Lord make a new thing, and the earth open her mouth, and swallow them up, with all that appertain unto them, and they go down quick into the pit; then ye shall understand that these men have provoked the Lord" (vv. 28-30).

Those were strong words, but Korah and his followers had committed a gross sin. They failed to realize that their position among the Israelites was appointed by God and that they were to be content in that position, just as Moses had been appointed by God and was to be content in his position. This truth is especially seen during the Church Age, because God has placed believers in the Body to perform specific functions. First Corinthians 12 discusses at length how believers need each other and how they must work together properly if they are to honor the Lord.

Moses made the real issue clear when he told Korah and his followers, "For which cause both thou and all thy company are gathered together against the Lord: and what is Aaron, that ye murmur against him?" (Num. 16:11). Always remember that an accusation against God's chosen one is a direct accusation against God Himself.

Moses declared that a unique judgment would fall on Korah and his men. If that judgment did not fall, then Moses was willing to admit that he was not God's leader. But when Moses finished speaking, "the earth opened her mouth, and swallowed them up, and their houses, and all the men that appertained unto Korah, and all their goods. They, and all that appertained to them, went down alive into the pit, and the earth closed upon them: and they perished from among the congregation" (vv. 32,33).

But notice the result of this judgment of God. The next day the Israelites "murmured against Moses and against Aaron, saying, Ye have killed the people of the Lord" (v. 41). Instead of teaching the Israelites a lesson, the judgment on Korah and his followers had only caused the Israelites to question God and to defend those who rebelled against Him. This was the lowest kind of ingratitude. The intercession of Moses and Aaron had saved the congregation from God's judgment, but these same people turned against their leaders after the death of the rebels.

The Lord told Moses, "Get you up from among this congregration, that I may consume them as in a moment" (v. 45). Before Moses and Aaron could intercede and make atonement for the people, a plague struck which killed 14,700 (see vv. 46-49). Moses and Aaron had been accused by the Israelites of being murderers. But they were really the saviors of the people, for had they not interceded, all would have been destroyed.

All of this resulted because of the rebellion of Korah and those who followed him. The awfulness of their sin can be measured by the penalty God inflicted on them.

Consider the ways that Moses' character manifested itself under such pressure. First, Moses let God vindicate him as the chosen leader, along with Aaron. Moses did not defend himself before those who challenged his position.

Second, even though the people opposed him, Moses interceded to save these same people from the wrath of God, and a great multitude owed their lives to him.

Third, although Moses interceded for the people, he did not shirk his God-given responsibility as a leader. He stood firm in his position; he did not run away and give up. He stood still and let God do the fighting.

Fourth, although he was personally challenged, Moses handled these incidents in such a way that the people were struck with awe and fear toward God. Moses magnified God rather than himself.

Chapter 7

Kadesh-Barnea: Place of Decision

After the time of Miriam's purification from the leprosy God brought upon her, "the people removed from Hazeroth, and pitched in the wilderness of Paran" (Num. 12:16). The wilderness of Paran was south of the land of Palestine. As the Israelites journeyed toward the Promised Land, it was necessary for them to go through the wilderness of Paran. At the northern edge of this wilderness was a place known both as "Kadesh" and "Kadesh-barnea." Kadesh-barnea was just south of the Promised Land and figured prominently in Israel's history. From this place the spies were sent into the land of Canaan and then returned "unto the wilderness of Paran, to Kadesh; and brought back word unto them" (13:26).

The Israelites and the Believer

In Israel's history Kadesh-barnea became much more than a stopping place; it became a place of decision. A study of the history of Israel reveals many parallels that can be drawn to the individual believer in the present age. This is especially true of Israel's travels from Egypt to Canaan. Israel came out of Egyptian captivity, passed through the wilderness and eventually entered the land. This parallels an individual as he passes through his spiritual training period. Believers often reveal carnality during this important phase of life.

The natural state of an individual is mentioned in I Corinthians 2:14: "The natural man receiveth not the things of the Spirit of God: for they are foolishness unto him: neither can he know them, because they are spiritually discerned." The "natural man" is the person who has not trusted in Jesus Christ as his personal Saviour. This parallels the Israelites in Egypt before they were saved by the blood of the lamb.

The Bible refers to carnal believers in I Corinthians 3:1: "And I, brethren, could not speak unto you as unto spiritual, but as unto carnal, even as unto babes in Christ." These were believers because they were "in Christ." However, they were immature believers who were being trained in the spiritual walk and for spiritual warfare. It is a characteristic of immature Christians to long for the things of the world, just as the Israelites in the wilderness longed for the things in Egypt.

The spiritual believer is referred to in I Corinthians 2:15: "He that is spiritual judgeth all things, yet he himself is judged of no man." This compares to the Israelites when they finally entered the land and claimed their rightful possessions.

Thus we see that three stages often occur in a believer's life, although not every believer goes through a lengthy time in the carnal stage. It is important, however, for the individual believer to study Israel's history and to learn valuable lessons. Concerning the Old Testament experiences of Israel, I Corinthians 10:6 says, "Now these things happened as examples for us, that we should not crave evil things, as they also craved" (NASB). Verse 11 says, "Now these things happened to them as an example, and they were written for our instruction, upon whom the ends of the ages have come" (NASB).

The Book of Hebrews emphasizes these same truths: "But with whom was he grieved forty years? Was it not with them that had sinned, whose carcases fell in the wilderness? And to whom sware he that they should not enter into his rest, but to them that believed not? So we see that they could not enter in because of unbelief. Let us therefore fear, lest, a promise being left us of entering into his rest, any of you should seem to come short of it" (3:17—4:1). Hebrews 4:9 says, "There remaineth therefore a rest to the people of God." Verse 10 adds, "For he that is entered into his rest, he also hath ceased from his own works, as God did from his."

Hebrews 4 refers to the need of the believer to rest in Jesus Christ even though he is walking on earth. The believer is to quit trying to accomplish things in his own strength and to accept by faith what Jesus Christ has for him and wants to do in and through him. The scriptural injunction to the believer concerning Israel is: "Let us labour [be diligent] therefore to enter into that rest, lest any man fall after the same example of unbelief" (v. 11).

Kadesh-barnea became a place with special meaning for the Israelites because the course of their history was changed there. That is why it is proper to speak of Kadesh-barnea as a place of decision.

The way the name "Kadesh-barnea" is used concerning Israel is comparable to the way the word "waterloo" is commonly used today. Inasmuch as Napoleon was defeated at Waterloo, it is now common to refer to a person's defeat as his waterloo. Because of what happened to Israel at Kadesh-barnea, it is also valid to refer to an individual believer's being at his Kadesh-barnea; that is, at the place of decision.

The believer must decide whether to remain at Kadesh-barnea in the desert and the place of defeat or to rest in Jesus Christ and go on to maturity, just as Israel eventually entered the land. The choice is up to the individual believer; no one can make it for him. Each person who knows Christ as Saviour must decide whether he will remain in the place of spiritual infancy and defeat or go on to the place of victory and spiritual maturity.

The Israelites had been delivered from Egypt by the blood of the lamb and had been separated from Egypt by the Red Sea. This set up the potential for their entrance into Canaan. What God had done for the people was so well known that even other nations feared the Israelites (see Josh. 2:9-11).

God had provided for Israel in the desert by giving a cloud to protect and to guide, manna for food and water for drink. He also protected them from enemies such as Amalek. The people were given the Law and were organized into a great commonwealth.

By the time the Israelites arrived at Kadesh-barnea, about two years had elapsed since they had crossed the Red Sea.

Those two years had been spent in training so they would learn to walk by faith and to be ready to do spiritual warfare in Canaan. So as they stood at Kadesh-barnea, they were faced with a great test—they had to decide whether or not they would take God at His word and walk and conquer by faith. They had to decide whether or not they would go on to spiritual victory.

Canaan and the Believer

It is important to note that Canaan does not represent heaven, as some songs indicate. Canaan was a place of warfare and provides a parallel to the spiritual warfare engaged in by the believer. The believer's spiritual warfare is detailed in Ephesians 6:10-18. This is really the abundant life that Christ spoke of in John 10:10: "I am come that they might have life, and that they might have it more abundantly."

Rather than thinking of Canaan as an illustration of heaven, it is more accurate to think of it as representing life "in the heavenlies" while the believer is here on earth. The Book of Ephesians—commonly considered the New Testament counterpart to the Old Testament Book of Joshua—says much about the believer's life in the heavenlies. The Apostle Paul was used of God to write Ephesians, and he said, "Blessed be the God and Father of our Lord Jesus Christ, who hath blessed us with all spiritual blessings in heavenly places in Christ" (1:3). Paul also said that God "hath raised us up together, and made us sit together in heavenly places in Christ Jesus" (2:6). The phrase "in heavenly places" in both of these verses is a reference to the heavenlies.

The believer who lives on the basis of his position in the heavenly realm is characterized by an abundant life. Second Peter 1:3 reveals that God has made everything available that is necessary for the believer to live this abundant life: "[He] hath given unto us all things that pertain unto life and godliness."

So Canaan really stands for the victorious Christian experience that is possible for the believer here and now. Kadesh-barnea represents the place of decision the believer comes to as he progresses spiritually in this life.

The Desert and the Believer

A present-day believer who has a wildernesslike Christian life is similar to the Israelites in the desert. They wandered here and there without a special sense of direction. It is easy for a Christian today to be caught up in the routine and not have any sense of direction about what he should be doing. Even local churches can have programs only for the sake of programs without really having a purpose in mind that produces something beneficial in the believer's life.

A Christian in the midst of a wilderness experience is not a fruitful Christian, just as Israel led a fruitless life in the desert. The Israelites were characterized by unbelief which expressed itself in their lives through doubt, frustration and complaining. They did not have the confidence in God to realize that He was using adverse circumstances to accomplish something for their good. Romans 8:28 specifically states this truth: "We know that all things work together for good to them that love God, to them who are the called according to his purpose."

In the wilderness Israel's main virtue was a negative one—they were not doing what the Egyptians were doing (although they secretly longed to do those things). There was nothing positive or spiritually aggressive about the life of Israel while in the desert.

Many Christians today are like the Israelites of old—they are characterized by a negative position rather than a positive one. They do not drink, dance, smoke, swear, cheat or lie. But after listing what they do not do, it is sometimes very difficult to see any positive elements in their lives. One often looks in vain for aggressive spiritual warriors. Believers are told, "Finally, my brethren, be strong in the Lord, and in the power of his might" (Eph. 6:10).

The reality of the spiritual warfare of the believer is seen in Ephesians 6:12: "For we wrestle not against flesh and blood, but against principalities, against powers, against the rulers of the darkness of this world, against spiritual wickedness in high places." Instructions for this spiritual warfare include directions to put on the whole armor of God so that the believer will be able to stand victoriously (vv. 13-17). In addition, the believer is to be "praying always with all prayer and supplication in the Spirit, and watching thereunto with all perseverance and supplication for all saints" (v. 18).

Each believer needs to ask himself if he is still wandering around in the desert or if he is really engaged in spiritual warfare with the Lord. We must wage spiritual war against the evil forces that keep souls bound and blinded. We who know Christ as Saviour need to demonstrate positive lives through prayer, the teaching of the Word, personal testimony and the help we give in whatever way we can.

The nation of Israel was useless to God as long as it lived in the wilderness. God did not forsake them, but they were useless in the sense that they were not accomplishing anything for Him. So, too, Christians today who live on the wilderness plane of life accomplish little, if anything, for God. The exhortation to such believers is: "Therefore leaving the elementary teaching about the Christ, let us press on to maturity, not laying again a foundation of repentance from dead works and of faith toward God" (Heb. 6:1, NASB).

At Kadesh-barnea Israel was at a crucial point in its national life. Two years had passed since the people had been redeemed from Egypt, and the land they had long dreamed of was before them. Kadesh-barnea was essentially the gateway to the land of Canaan.

The land of Canaan had been an important focus of their thinking for many years. God had promised Abraham seed, or descendants, and a land more than 400 years earlier (see Gen. 12:1-3). The promises of seed and land always go together, but the descendants of Abraham had been separated from the land for many years.

Egypt had been used by God for a special purpose in the life of Israel. In Egypt the Israelites were put by themselves because the Egyptians would not intermarry with them. But finally, Pharaoh's power over the Israelites had been broken, and Israel was on its way to the Promised Land.

At Kadesh-barnea the nation faced an hour of crisis. The people were at a place of great decision. This was the greatest moment for that generation of Israelites.

To go forward would mean immediate possession with no Jordan River to cross, no more years of desert wandering and no death in the wilderness because of disobedience. What would their decision be? Would they enter the land? Israel stood at the moment of destiny with untold potential. A mistake here would cast the die and mark the course for future generations and would cause them to think of the past and what might have been. And as John Greenleaf Whittier said, "For of all sad words of tongue or pen, the saddest are these: 'It might have been!' "

A New Testament Passage

Before examining what happened to the Israelites at Kadesh-barnea, consider a New Testament passage that has been frequently misunderstood by many believers. It relates to the subject of deciding about going on to maturity, and that is why it is important to consider this passage in connection with the decision that faced Israel.

The passage is in the Book of Hebrews. This book emphasizes the need for the believer to go on to maturity. Early in the book the writer asks, "How shall we escape, if we neglect so great salvation?" (2:3). The reference is not to unbelievers but to believers. The entire Book of Hebrews was addressed to Hebrew Christians. The author was concerned that believers go on to a salvation characterized by maturity and not stop with a salvation that only delivers from condemnation.

As the author developed his theme, he referred to Melchizedek and then made statements that are highly significant for every believer who desires to go on to maturity. Writing by inspiration of God, he said, "Of whom we have many things to say, and hard to be uttered, seeing ye are dull of hearing. For when for the time ye ought to be teachers, ye have need that one teach you again which be the first principles of the oracles of God; and are become such as have need of milk, and not of strong meat. For every one that useth milk is unskilful in the word of righteousness: for he is a babe. But strong meat belongeth to them that are of full age, even those who by reason of use have their senses exercised to discern both good and evil. Therefore leaving the principles of the doctrine of Christ, let us go on unto perfection; not laying again the foundation of repentance from dead works, and of faith toward God" (5:11—6:1).

Then follow the difficult verses that so many stumble over: "For it is impossible for those who were once enlightened, and have tasted of the heavenly gift, and were made partakers of the Holy Ghost, and have tasted the good word of God, and the powers of the world to come, if they shall fall away, to renew them again unto repentance; seeing they crucify to themselves the Son of God afresh, and put him to an open shame" (vv. 4-6).

The writer of Hebrews made it clear in 5:11-14 that, at a time when the Christians to whom he was writing should be teaching others, they themselves needed to be taught. In effect he was saying, "You need to be taught again the ABCs of God's revelation to mankind." They were unable to take solid spiritual food, and the indication is that anyone who is unable to take solid food is immature.

Having said that, the writer of Hebrews said, "Therefore leaving the principles of the doctrine of Christ, let us go on unto perfection; not laying again the foundation of repentance from dead works, and of faith toward God" (6:1). In other words, it was not necessary to again lay foundational truths since they had already been laid. The believer is not to continue to dwell on the gospel and its foundational truths. Having trusted Jesus Christ as personal Saviour, he is then to go on to maturity. A believer who remains at the gospel stage is immature. Having once received spiritual life, he needs the food of God's Word in order to go on to maturity.

But what about those controversial verses that say a person cannot be renewed to repentance if he falls away? I personally believe the author is talking about believers, for he refers to them as having been "once enlightened" and having "tasted of the heavenly gift" (v. 4). He also says they "were made partakers of the Holy Ghost" (v. 4). Also, they had "tasted the good word of God, and the powers of the world to come" (v. 5).

The writer was saying that, for those who have experienced salvation, it is impossible for them to be renewed to repentance as they were when they first trusted Christ for salvation. For them to even think of such would be to recrucify the Son of God in their minds and expose Him to shame and contempt by their conduct. A person cannot be born again over and over again.

Even though this is a complex passage, let us consider what it does not teach. Some are under the impression that it teaches the possibility that a believer can lose his salvation; that is, he can "fall away" from his salvation. Although many believe this, none is able to say precisely how much sin it takes to cause a falling away from salvation. Is it one sin or two or three or more? Or does it have to do with how gross the sin is? But then, is not one sin just as bad as another in the eyes of God?

Those who believe this passage teaches that a believer can lose his salvation usually do not emphasize what the rest of the passage says—that once he falls away, it is impossible to renew him again. This would mean that the person who lost his salvation could never again be saved. Who, then, is really saved? Have not all believers at one time or another fallen into sin?

But I believe the entire Book of Hebrews was written to Christians to tell them how to go on to a mature Christian life. What the author was writing about in Hebrews 6 was not the matter of losing one's salvation but of going on to maturity. The words "fall away" in verse 6 refer to those who refuse to go on with God into a life of maturity. So when a believer realizes his need of going on to maturity and deliberately opposes doing so, he cannot be renewed to repentance; that is, he then forfeits his opportunity to go on to maturity.

By refusing to go into the land, Israel was refusing to go on to spiritual maturity. This was a deliberate act of unbelief and a rejection of God's continuing purpose for them. This refusal denied God's ability to complete what He had promised, even though the nation had seen Him perform many miracles in its behalf. So Hebrews 6 refers to going on to spiritual maturity, a maturity found only in the risen and ascended Christ. The people to whom this passage was written were already believers, and Jesus Himself said concerning believers, "I give unto them eternal life; and they shall never perish, neither shall any man pluck them out of my hand. My Father, which gave them me, is greater than all;

and no man is able to pluck them out of my Father's hand" (John 10:28,29).

What a shame, however, that, although some know Jesus Christ as personal Saviour, their lives are characterized by a refusal to really take God at His word in daily living. These do not go on to spiritual maturity. The Old Testament includes many lessons for these people to learn, and that is why we focus attention on the Israelites as they stood at Kadesh-barnea, ready to enter the land of Canaan. Would they believe God and keep moving forward, or would they be characterized by unbelief and refuse to go any farther? The latter would be a deliberate act of unbelief and a refusal to accept their better knowledge.

Israel Asks for Spies

Rather than going into the land immediately, the Israelites called for spies to be sent in first. The Bible says, "The Lord spake unto Moses, saying, Send thou men, that they may search the land of Canaan, which I give unto the children of Israel: of every tribe of their fathers shall ye send a man, every one a ruler among them" (Num. 13:1,2).

If these are the only two verses one reads on this subject, he might think that the Lord wanted the spies to be sent into Canaan, and this would absolve the Israelites from responsibility. Comparison with another passage of scripture indicates otherwise, however. Several years later, when Moses was rehearsing for the Israelites what had taken place at Kadesh-barnea, he gave additional information concerning this incident. Actually, his review took place 38 years later, and the Israelites were only then getting ready to enter the land. But before they entered Canaan, Moses reminded them of what had taken place back at Kadesh-barnea.

"And when we departed from Horeb, we went through all that great and terrible wilderness, which ye saw by the way of the mountain of the Amorites, as the Lord our God commanded us; and we came to Kadesh-barnea. And I said unto you, Ye are come unto the mountain of the Amorites, which the Lord our God doth give unto us. Behold, the Lord thy God hath set the land before thee: go up and possess it, as the Lord God of thy fathers hath said unto thee; fear not, neither be discouraged. And ye came near unto me every one of you, and said, We will send men before us, and they shall search us out the land, and bring us word again by what way we must go up, and into what cities we shall come. And the saying pleased me well: and I took twelve men of you, one of a tribe" (Deut. 1:19-23).

Notice in particular that Moses said the Israelites asked for these spies to be sent in and that he agreed with them. It is apparent that God had not wanted the Israelites to send spies into the land; He wanted them to take Him at His word and go in by faith. But because the people wanted the spies to see what the land was like, God granted permission for this to be done.

This reveals a distinction between God's direct will and His permissive will. This distinction is frequently found in the Scriptures. God permits some things simply because of the hardness of peoples' hearts. Because of Israel's unbelief, God was longsuffering with them along the way. That is why God permitted them to send spies into the land, even though He did not want them to do so. This reveals that the people were characterized by unbelief. Even though God had enabled them to overcome the greatest nation in the world at that time (Egypt), they could not trust Him to overcome the much smaller nations in the land of Canaan.

In addition to being characterized by unbelief, the Israelites were also characterized by self-will. Concerning the Israelites, the psalmist said, "They quickly forgot His works; they did not wait for His counsel, but craved intensely in the wilderness, and tempted God in the desert. So He gave them their request, but sent a wasting disease among them" (Ps. 106:13-15, NASB). The King James Version translates this last verse: "He gave them their request; but sent leanness into their soul" (v. 15). This reveals that God sometimes permits what is not in His direct will. It also reveals that the individual loses out spiritually.

What a paradox! The Israelites were to walk by faith, but they wanted to send spies into the land. What does faith want with spies? Apparently they were more concerned about walking by sight than by faith.

Many believers today find it extremely difficult to take God at His word. Instead of walking by faith, they want proofs about the future beyond what God has said and the power He has demonstrated. They are just like the Israelites who wanted to send spies into the land so they would know what it was like and how strong it was. Then they would choose whether or not to go in. Every believer should remember II Corinthians 5:7: "(For we walk by faith, not by sight.)"

God's Promises

God knew the difficulties that Israel would face, and He knew how to surmount them. Had He not proven this during the two years since the Israelites left Egypt? Even while they were in Egypt, God had made a promise and then kept it: "I will bring you out from under the burdens of the Egyptians, and I will rid you out of their bondage, and I will redeem you with a stretched out arm, and with great judgments: and I will take you to me for a people, and I will be to you a God: and ye shall know that I am the Lord your God, which bringeth you out from under the burdens of the Egyptians. And I will bring you in unto the land, concerning the which I did swear to give it to Abraham, to Isaac, and to Jacob; and I will give it you for an heritage: I am the Lord" (Ex. 6:6-8).

God had promised to deliver them out of the land (v. 6). Had He not done so? He had promised to take them to Himself (v. 7). Had He not done so? He had promised to bring them into the land (v. 8). What would keep Him from fulfilling this promise also?

What an application exists here for present-day believers! Remember, the land of Canaan, as it parallels the Christian's life, refers to involvement in spiritual warfare. As such, it is a parallel of the abundant life that God wants every believer to have (see John 10:10). Just as God had accomplished things for Israel in the past and was also able to do so in the future, God is able to bring the present-day believer into a victorious life.

Philippians 1:6 says to the believer, "Being confident of this very thing, that he which hath begun a good work in you will perform it until the day of Jesus Christ." God had begun a good work in Israel, and He was able to give them all they needed in the future. Why did they need spies? And God has provided salvation for all who believe, so once an individual comes into right relationship with Him, he is to walk in reliance on God, not on the basis of sight.

If you know Jesus Christ as your Saviour, God has begun a good work in you, and He is able to perfect it. But, of course, He needs your cooperation of faith. God will not override your will to bring you to the place of spiritual maturity. But any believer who does not go on to spiritual maturity cannot blame a lack of God's provisions for this. Second Peter 1:3 clearly reveals that God has made available all we need for "life and godliness."

Romans 8:31,32 also reveals the marvelous way God works in behalf of a believer: "What shall we then say to these things? If God be for us, who can be against us? He that spared not his own Son, but delivered him up for us all, how shall he not with him also freely give us all things?" No wonder verse 37 says, "In all these things we are more than conquerors through him that loved us." Because of all that God has done for us and has made possible for us, let us go on to maturity by trusting Him all the way.

God is faithful to His Word. There is no need to doubt the wonderful promises He has made. Numbers 23:19 says, "God is not a man, that he should lie; neither the son of man, that he should repent: hath he said, and shall he not do it? Or hath he spoken, and shall he not make it good?" This is the kind of wonderful God we have!

Our God is the same God that Israel had. Instead of trusting Him and believing His word, they demanded that spies be sent into the land first. Such a demand was equivalent to saying that they could not believe God or trust His power to enable them to overcome any obstacle they would find. They thought it was necessary first to know for sure what God was talking about. They evidenced a tremendous lack of faith.

Instead of taking God at His word, they thought they had to confirm it by man's approval. And this same thing often happens today. The Lord burdens an individual to do a particular thing, but he sometimes refuses to begin without first getting man's approval.

True faith interprets circumstances through a realization of who God is. As one truly knows God, he will realize that circumstances amount to nothing. Weak faith (which is actually unbelief) must be bolstered by human investigation and visible proof. This is why there is such an emphasis today on experience—believers are unwilling to take God at His word. True faith looks from God to the circumstances, which erases all questions. On the other hand, weak faith shuts out God and sees only the difficulty. It creates a multitude of unanswered questions.

Israel seemed to be wary of entire dependence on God; they wished to think for themselves and act on their own reasoning. But as II Corinthians 3:5 says, "Not that we are fit (qualified and sufficient in ability) of ourselves to form personal judgments or to claim or count anything as coming from us; but our power and ability and sufficiency are from God" (Amplified).

In reality, the spies which Israel sent into the land of Canaan investigated in order to verify divine truthfulness. They set themselves up as judges of God. But true faith takes God at His word.

Two years of training with God was sufficient to prove Him, but the people stubbornly resisted the clear word of God and disbelieved. Notice God's reaction to the Israelites' unbelief: "But with whom was he grieved forty years? Was it not with them that had sinned, whose carcases fell in the wilderness? And to whom sware he that they should not enter into his rest, but to them that believed not? So we see that they could not enter in because of unbelief" (Heb. 3:17-19).

True faith rests in the Person of Christ. Hebrews 11:6 says, "But without faith it is impossible to please him: for he that cometh to God must believe that he is, and that he is a rewarder of them that diligently seek him."

The Report of the Spies

Moses chose an individual from each of the 12 tribes and sent the men to spy out the land of Canaan. They spied out the land for 40 days and then returned to give their report. "They went and came to Moses, and to Aaron, and to all the

congregation of the children of Israel, unto the wilderness of
Paran, to Kadesh; and brought back word unto them, and
unto all the congregation, and shewed them the fruit of the
land. And they told him, and said, We came unto the land
whither thou sentest us, and surely it floweth with milk and
honey; and this is the fruit of it. Nevertheless the people be
strong that dwell in the land, and the cities are walled, and
very great: and moreover we saw the children of Anak there.
The Amalekites dwell in the land of the south: and the
Hittites, and the Jebusites, and the Amorites, dwell in the
mountains: and the Canaanites dwell by the sea, and by the
coast of Jordan" (Num. 13:26-29).

The spies first verified God's word concerning the worth
of the land. They described it as a place flowing with milk
and honey and even displayed samples of the fruit they
brought back. How interesting that they had verified what
God had said and what they previously had been unable to
believe. They had seen the productivity of the land, so they
were no longer taking it by faith but by sight.

Ten of the 12 spies gave a glowing report of the
productivity of the land but added a "nevertheless" when
they referred to the people living there (v. 28). This indicates
that they were looking at circumstances, because a person
looking from God to circumstances never says
"nevertheless." But as these spies gave their report, they
indicated their lack of faith in God. They had seen the giants
in the land, and because the spies were afraid of them, they
thought God would not be able to overcome them. They
were interpreting everything in the light of their own
experience rather than interpreting everything on the basis of
who God is.

How common this fallacy is among believers today; they
base almost everything on experience instead of on the Word
of God. The conclusion of the ten spies was: "We be not able
to go up against the people; for they are stronger than we"
(v. 31). But notice that their report is referred to as "an evil
report" (v. 32). The spies, of course, did not think it was an
evil report; they considered it to be a wise, carefully thought
out report. They said, "The land, through which we have
gone to search it, is a land that eateth up the inhabitants
thereof; and all the people that we saw in it are men of a

great stature. And there we saw the giants, the sons of Anak, which come of the giants: and we were in our own sight as grasshoppers, and so we were in their sight" (vv. 32,33).

Notice that in their report the spies said, "All the people that we saw in it are men of a great stature" (v. 32). That was not really true. Although they might have seen many of great stature, not all of them were giants. But this only shows that the spies' hearts were filled with fear, which greatly influenced their interpretation of everything.

The spies were so overwhelmed by the people of the land that they said, "We were in our own sight as grasshoppers, and so we were in their sight" (v. 33). The obstacles looked overwhelming because the spies were interpreting everything from a human viewpoint.

The Report of Caleb and Joshua

But not all of the spies were guilty of unbelief. Two of them, Caleb and Joshua, did not agree with the report of the others. "Caleb stilled the people before Moses, and said, Let us go up at once, and possess it; for we are well able to overcome it" (Num. 13:30).

What a different report! Joshua and Caleb had seen the same difficulties as the other spies, but the key difference was their faith. Faith brings God into the picture; unbelief shuts Him out. The way that God's power is kept from operating by unbelief is clearly seen in the report of the ten spies. They surely had been at the Red Sea when God opened it, allowed Israel to pass through and then closed it to destroy the armies of the greatest nation in the world. But because of the unbelief of these spies, they had such a small God that they appeared to be grasshoppers in the eyes of others.

How big is your God? It is easy to sing "How great Thou art," but it is quite another thing to believe this when faced with difficult circumstances. An observer might think that some of us should sing, "How small Thou art." This was especially true of the spies who fixed their attention on the circumstances rather than on God.

Notice what the spies were trusting in—the military might of the nation. When they saw the inhabitants of the land and then considered their own military might, the spies decided they were unable to take the land. Because they saw things only from a human viewpoint, their eyes were fixed on the walled cities and the giants. Unbelief never looks beyond the circumstances.

Faith, on the other hand, although it never minimizes the difficulties after seeing them, looks into the face of God and relies on Him. But because faith looks first at God, it sees the difficulties to be extremely small by comparison.

So, in contrast to the negative report of the ten spies, Joshua and Caleb gave a positive report. When the Israelites heard the reports, they believed the negative report and were so discouraged they wanted to appoint a captain and return to Egypt (14:4). Moses and Aaron were horrified by such a thought, and they fell on their faces before the Israelites (v. 5). Joshua and Caleb tore their clothes as they heard such unbelief expressed, and they told the people, "The land, which we passed through to search it, is an exceeding good land. If the Lord delight in us, then he will bring us into this land, and give it us; a land which floweth with milk and honey. Only rebel not ye against the Lord, neither fear ye the people of the land; for they are bread for us: their defence is departed from them, and the Lord is with us: fear them not" (vv. 7-9).

The unbelieving spies considered the inhabitants of the land to be giants, but as Joshua and Caleb looked at them, they considered them to be "bread for us" (v. 9). In other words, Joshua and Caleb's faith was so great that they thought the Israelites would eat up the inhabitants of the land just as a person eats bread. But notice that they placed one condition on such a victory: "if the Lord delight in us" (v. 8). Their confidence was in the Lord, not in military might.

Joshua and Caleb made it clear as to why military might was not the real consideration: "Their defence is departed from them, and the Lord is with us: fear them not" (v. 9). Joshua 2 indicates why the people were defenseless. Rahab shared with two spies (sent into the land at a later time) that the people had been living in fear of the Israelites ever since they had heard about their crossing the Red Sea and their victory over other armies (see vv. 10,11).

Numbers 13 and 14 makes it evident that ten of the spies interpreted God in light of circumstances, whereas the other two spies (Joshua and Caleb) interpreted circumstances in light of God. Because of the faith Joshua and Caleb had in God, they said, "Let us go up at once," and, "We are well able to overcome it" (13:30). Do you wonder how you will be able to overcome the obstacles in your life? If you know Jesus Christ as your Saviour, I John 4:4 applies directly to you: "Greater is he that is in you, than he that is in the world." This is why the Apostle Paul said, "Christ in you, the hope of glory" (Col. 1:27). Certainly the walls of circumstances will be high, but God is even higher. Certainly the giants are strong, but God is stronger—He is almighty.

Faith is not indifferent nor is it reckless; rather, it looks the difficulty straight in the face because it has seen God and draws strength from Him. Therefore believers are told, "Be strong in the Lord, and in the power of his might" (Eph. 6:10). To faith there is never a wall too high, never a city too great and never a giant too strong.

Reaction of the Israelites

Notice what happened when Joshua and Caleb took a strong stand for the Lord: "All the congregation bade stone them with stones" (Num. 14:10). Think of it—the people wanted to kill the only two spies who had any confidence in God! This is often how fickle even believers become. They react to those who really take God at His word and want to move ahead.

If God had not promised to bring the people into the land, He might have destroyed them completely right there. And if it were not for the grace of God, He might immediately destroy some people today who disregard the complete salvation they have. For instance, those who are unconcerned about having an abundant life show total disregard for the words of Christ: "I am come that they might have life, and that they might have it more abundantly" (John 10:10).

And some refuse to take God at His word concerning the security that each believer has in Christ. The Lord Jesus

Christ said, "My sheep hear my voice, and I know them, and they follow me: and I give unto them eternal life; and they shall never perish, neither shall any man pluck them out of my hand. My Father, which gave them me, is greater than all; and no man is able to pluck them out of my Father's hand" (vv. 27-29). Those who claim they can take themselves out of the hand of God are actually implying that they are greater than God. Concerning salvation, the Bible promises, "He which hath begun a good work in you will perform it until the day of Jesus Christ" (Phil. 1:6).

Do not misunderstand. Just because a believer is secure in Christ does not mean he should willfully sin. The Apostle Paul dealt with this very subject in the Book of Romans. He said, "That as sin hath reigned unto death, even so might grace reign through righteousness unto eternal life by Jesus Christ our Lord. What shall we say then? Shall we continue in sin, that grace may abound? God forbid. How shall we that are dead to sin, live any longer therein?" (5:21—6:2).

In Galatians the Apostle Paul told believers, "For, brethren, ye have been called unto liberty; only use not liberty for an occasion to the flesh, but by love serve one another" (5:13). Believers are told in I Peter 2:16, "As free, and not using your liberty for a cloke of maliciousness, but as the servants of God."

The person who has experienced the regenerating work of the Holy Spirit in his life will not want to sin even though he will often sin. The Holy Spirit lives within the believer (I Cor. 6:19), and He convicts the person of sin when it is committed. Those who do not confess their sin at first sometimes have to go through severe chastening (see Heb. 12:8-11) before they come to their spiritual senses and confess their sin to God. And believers are promised: "If we confess our sins, he is faithful and just to forgive us our sins, and to cleanse us from all unrighteousness" (I John 1:9).

It is hard to believe that the Israelites wanted to stone Joshua and Caleb for telling them the truth about God. But Joshua and Caleb were experiencing a principle stated in II Timothy 3:12: "All who desire to live godly in Christ Jesus will be persecuted" (NASB). If we live according to man-made rules, we will be applauded for our

accomplishments. But when we renounce all dependence on
our own ability, testify to God's grace and depend only on
Him, we will suffer persecution.

Chapter 8

Kadesh-Barnea: Result of Decision

The report of the ten spies influenced the course of the entire nation of Israel. When the spies gave the glowing report about the land and added their "nevertheless" (Num. 13:28), the people became as filled with fear as the spies. "All the congregation lifted up their voice, and cried; and the people wept that night" (14:1). This is a good example of the fact that the opinion of relatively few (actually ten) can have a significant influence on a multitude (about three million people). The New Testament refers to the way an individual affects others: "For none of us liveth to himself, and no man dieth to himself" (Rom. 14:7). What a solemn responsibility each person has before God and man! It is exceedingly important that we be true and full of faith in what we say and do in our relationships with others and with God.

Reaction to the Positive Report

As so often is the case today, the negative report of the spies carried more weight with the Israelites than the positive report. Caleb quieted the people to give them his message: "Let us go up at once, and possess it; for we are well able to overcome it" (Num. 13:30). But although the people were quiet while Caleb spoke, they soon broke into loud crying because they believed the report of the ten spies rather than that of Caleb and Joshua. Mob psychology took over, even as it did when Christ entered Jerusalem in what is commonly referred to as His Triumphal Entry (see Matt. 21:1-11). Although many acclaimed Him as Messiah at that time, the official leadership of Judaism rejected Him, and a few days later the cry was "Crucify him, crucify him" (Luke 23:21).

After the ten spies had given their evil report, "all the congregation lifted up their voice, and cried; and the people wept that night" (Num. 14:1). They were frightened and discouraged by the report of these ten spies, and true faith seemed to find no place in them. They gave up all hope of ever entering the land of Canaan.

The Israelites "murmured against Moses and against Aaron: and the whole congregation said unto them, Would God that we had died in the land of Egypt! Or would God we had died in this wilderness!" (v. 2). What utter despair they were in! These who had witnessed such great miracles of God had no confidence in Him for the future and even wished they were dead.

They asked, "Wherefore hath the Lord brought us unto this land, to fall by the sword, that our wives and our children should be a prey? Were it not better for us to return into Egypt?" (v. 3). They even blamed God for the progress they had made up to that time. Had it not been for God, they would not have made it that far, but they did not remember this. Note especially that they were concerned about their wives and children. They were concerned about their little ones, but we will see later that these were the ones included in God's promise for the future and that God preserved.

The Israelites were so discouraged that they said, "Let us make a captain, and let us return into Egypt" (v. 4). God would never have allowed them to do that. In His great mercy and grace He had broken Egypt's power over them, and under no circumstances would He have allowed them to return to Egypt.

Their sin was not merely despair and despondency but outright unbelief that accused God of wrongdoing. This is evident from what Moses said later when he was reviewing Israel's history. Moses reminded the people, "Notwithstanding ye would not go up, but rebelled against the commandment of the Lord your God: and ye murmured in your tents, and said, Because the Lord hated us, he hath brought us forth out of the land of Egypt, to deliver us into the hand of the Amorites, to destroy us" (Deut. 1:26,27).

God had lovingly and mightily led them out of Egypt, but the people accused Him of hating them. How low can people sink in unbelief?

The men who led the people to this state of mind and decision were not to influence Israel anymore. Their judgment was quickly sealed by the Lord. Numbers 14:36,37 says, "And the men, which Moses sent to search the land, who returned, and made all the congregation to murmur against him, by bringing up a slander upon the land, even those men that did bring up the evil report upon the land, died by the plague before the Lord." This is a sobering reminder that "it is a fearful thing to fall into the hands of the living God" (Heb. 10:31).

Not only did the Israelites not believe God, but they also accused Him of thinking evil and wanting to do evil. How sad it is when a person comes to this low state. This is sometimes the case with those who lose loved ones—they become so embittered that they even accuse God of not loving them.

A Final Appeal

After the ten spies gave their evil report, which was believed by the people, God's men—Moses, Aaron, Joshua and Caleb—knew that the people had passed the place of no return in their willful unbelief. In their rebellion the people had sealed their own doom by voting for retreat, even though they knew God's ability. Moses and Aaron "fell on their faces before all the assembly" (Num. 14:5), and Joshua and Caleb "rent their clothes" (v. 6). Joshua and Caleb told the people, "The land, which we passed through to search it, is an exceeding good land. If the Lord delight in us, then he will bring us into this land, and give it us; a land which floweth with milk and honey. Only rebel not ye against the Lord, neither fear ye the people of the land; for they are bread for us: their defence is departed from them, and the Lord is with us: fear them not" (vv. 7-9).

This was the final appeal that Joshua and Caleb made to the rebellious Israelites with the hope of reversing their decision not to enter the land. Joshua and Caleb did not yet fully realize how God viewed this terrible sin of unbelief.

The confidence of Joshua and Caleb was in the Lord, and

they knew that He was able to bring the Israelites into the land successfully. But when they finished speaking, "all the congregation bade stone them with stones" (v. 10). The people wanted to kill these men of God for telling them the truth.

This reveals that the people had passed the point of no return. They had deliberately sinned—by an act of the will they had turned against God. Even though they had seen many miracles performed for them by God, they rejected Him against better knowledge. They refused to go on with Him. This is where Hebrews 6 relates to this part of the history of Israel. The Israelites had been enlightened, had tasted of the heavenly gift, had been made partakers of the Holy Spirit, had tasted of the good word of God and of the powers of the world to come (Heb. 6:4,5). But after knowing and experiencing all this, if they refused to go on with the Lord, it would be impossible to renew them to repentance—they would never again be given the opportunity to make this decision.

I do not believe that either Numbers 14 or Hebrews 6 refers to salvation; rather, these chapters refer to a child of God going on with the Lord in a deeper relationship of maturity. The death spoken of later is not spiritual death but physical.

God's government is just. Israel shut God out in unbelief; therefore, when the people later attempted to go up against the Canaanites, they went alone because God refused to go with them. So it became a battle of giants against grasshoppers instead of giants against God. Since they abandoned God in unbelief, He abandoned them in their presumption.

God Speaks

As soon as the congregation wanted to stone those who told them the truth, "the glory of the Lord appeared in the tabernacle of the congregation before all the children of Israel" (Num. 14:10). How awesome this must have been! God had something to say to those who refused to take Him at His word, and His appearance was evident to all.

God told Moses, "How long will this people provoke me? And how long will it be ere they believe me, for all the signs which I have shewed among them? I will smite them with the pestilence, and disinherit them, and will make of thee a greater nation and mightier than they" (vv. 11,12). This was God's first announcement of the judgment that was to come on the Israelites because of their unbelief. The judgment for their unbelief was physical death and disinheritance, not loss of salvation. Their salvation was based on the blood shed back in Egypt, for it was there that they acted by faith and applied the blood according to God's instructions. But because of their unbelief they were to be judged by God.

The judgment on the Israelites was not a complete destruction of the nation. Notice that God again offered to make of Moses a great nation, just as He had earlier (see Ex. 32:10). In spite of such a significant offer, notice that Moses interceded for the people.

Moses told the Lord, "Then the Egyptians shall hear it, (for thou broughtest up this people in thy might from among them;) and they will tell it to the inhabitants of this land: for they have heard that thou Lord art among this people, that thou Lord art seen face to face, and that thy cloud standeth over them, and that thou goest before them, by daytime in a pillar of a cloud, and in a pillar of fire by night. Now if thou shalt kill all this people as one man, then the nations which have heard the fame of thee will speak, saying, Because the Lord was not able to bring this people into the land which he sware unto them, therefore he hath slain them in the wilderness. And now, I beseech thee, let the power of my Lord be great, according as thou hast spoken" (Num. 14:13-17).

Even though there would be extremely hard times ahead, Moses again made it clear that he chose to suffer affliction with the Israelites rather than to enjoy the pleasures of sin for a season (Heb. 11:25). Moses did not want to go into the land without the other Israelites.

Moses' intercession had two basic appeals. First, Moses did not want God to let the heathen nations have any basis for denying God's omnipotence. Moses reminded God that all nations knew He dwelt in the midst of the nation of Israel (v. 14). Moses pleaded that if God killed the people, it would indicate to other nations that He did not have the ability to bring Israel into the land of Canaan (v. 16).

Second, Moses pleaded on the basis of the greatness of God. Moses said, "Let the power of my Lord be great, according as thou hast spoken, saying, The Lord is longsuffering, and of great mercy, forgiving iniquity and transgression, and by no means clearing the guilty, visiting the iniquity of the fathers upon the children unto the third and fourth generation. Pardon, I beseech thee, the iniquity of this people according unto the greatness of thy mercy, and as thou hast forgiven this people, from Egypt even until now" (vv. 17-19).

This is another of the great intercessions of Moses—a man whom God had offered to make the head of a new nation. Moses was concerned about what others would say about God as well as how the character of God would be maligned. Moses wanted the greatness of God's mercy and grace to be evident to all through the pardoning of the Israelites.

The Lord answered Moses, "I have pardoned according to thy word: but as truly as I live, all the earth shall be filled with the glory of the Lord. Because all those men which have seen my glory, and my miracles, which I did in Egypt and in the wilderness, and have tempted me now these ten times, and have not hearkened to my voice; surely they shall not see the land which I sware unto their fathers, neither shall any of them that provoked me see it" (vv. 20-23). This pronouncement of God surely reminds us of Hebrews 6:4-6.

Judgment Announced

God pardoned the people, but justice had to be meted out. Because the people had refused to believe Him, they would not be able to enter the land of Canaan. They had tested the Lord in the wilderness ten different times, and this incident brought an end to God's longsuffering for that generation. Those ten incidents of testing had occurred during the two years after they left Egypt.

The older generation of Israelites would not see the land, but there were two exceptions—Caleb and Joshua. God said, "But my servant Caleb, because he had another spirit with him, and hath followed me fully, him will I bring into the land whereinto he went; and his seed shall possess it" (Num. 14:24). Later, Joshua was mentioned, when God told Moses to tell the people, "Doubtless ye shall not come into the land, concerning which I sware to make you dwell therein, save Caleb the son of Jephunneh, and Joshua the son of Nun" (v. 30).

The first announcement of judgment came when God made it clear that He would punish the people because of their disbelief (see vv. 11,12). The second announcement came when God told the older generation that none of them except Joshua and Caleb would see the land (see vv. 22-24,30). Then the third announcement of judgment was heard throughout all Israel.

The Lord said to Moses and Aaron, "How long shall I bear with this evil congregation, which murmur against me? I have heard the murmurings of the children of Israel, which they murmur against me. Say unto them, As truly as I live, saith the Lord, as ye have spoken in mine ears, so will I do to you: your carcases shall fall in this wilderness; and all that were numbered of you, according to your whole number, from twenty years old and upward, which have murmured against me" (vv. 27-29).

In addition to sparing Joshua and Caleb from this judgment, God also spared the younger generation. God said, "But your little ones, which ye said should be a prey, them will I bring in, and they shall know the land which ye have despised" (v. 31).

All over 20 who had seen God's great wonders but had refused to enter the land were to be destroyed in the wilderness. The only exceptions were Caleb and Joshua, who brought back a good report. Those under 20 were also to be spared and brought into the land. This younger generation was not responsible for the decision their parents made in refusing to enter the land.

What a shame that those who were 20 years old and older had to spend the next 38 years in aimless wandering in the desert, simply waiting to die. There was no inheritance for them. They did not lose their salvation, but they lost their inheritance. Because of their unbelief and failure to take God at His word, they led lives of fruitless misery.

God did not forsake them; He was with them even in

their desert experiences. He continued to provide the manna, the water and the cloud, but the hope of entering Canaan was lost forever to this generation. They were doomed to abide by their fateful decision in refusing to enter the land.

Even Joshua and Caleb, who dared to believe God, had to return to the wilderness with the others. Joshua and Caleb had to suffer along with them for 38 more years. This is an example of the way decisions affect other people. But the faith of Joshua and Caleb was characterized by great patience. Because they believed God, they were able to endure even the experiences of the desert without losing hope.

After God pronounced that none would enter the land except Joshua and Caleb and the younger generation, the Bible records God's judgment on the ten spies. They were judged by physical death right there and then. "The men, which Moses sent to search the land, who returned, and made all the congregation to murmur against him, by bringing up a slander upon the land, even those men that did bring up the evil report upon the land, died by the plague before the Lord" (Num. 14:36,37). Surely this judgment caused the others to realize that the Lord was not to be trifled with. This surely underscored in their minds that God expects to be taken at His word and not mocked by unbelief.

After Moses communicated to the people the messages of God, "the people mourned greatly. And they rose up early in the morning, and gat them up into the top of the mountain, saying, Lo, we be here, and will go up unto the place which the Lord hath promised: for we have sinned" (vv. 39,40).

Although they confessed their sin—at least with their lips if not with their heart—this did not keep them from reaping the results of their deliberate turning against God's leadership. They had sinned against better knowledge, and they were to suffer the consequences of it.

Israel's Sin of Presumption

Notice that, after they learned that the Lord would not let them go into the land, they made a rash decision to "go up unto the place which the Lord hath promised" (v. 40). Earlier, God had wanted them to do this, and they had refused; when God said they would not enter the land, they presumed to go anyway. This was simply adding one sin to another. Their sin of unbelief led them to the sin of presumption, as well as the sin of self-confidence.

Moses told them, "Wherefore now do ye transgress the commandment of the Lord? But it shall not prosper. Go not up, for the Lord is not among you; that ye be not smitten before your enemies" (vv. 41,42). Moses explained that the Amalekites and Canaanites would have to be faced and that the Israelites would fall by the sword because they had turned away from the Lord (v. 43). God was not going with them; He could not be mocked.

In spite of Moses' words of caution, however, "they presumed to go up unto the hill top: nevertheless the ark of the covenant of the Lord, and Moses, departed not out of the camp. Then the Amalekites came down, and the Canaanites which dwelt in that hill, and smote them, and discomfited them, even unto Hormah" (vv. 44,45). So we see what happens when people presume upon God's grace.

They had sinned by refusing to enter the land as God said they should; then they had sinned by presuming to go when He said they could not. The result was inevitable—they were driven back because God's blessing was not on them. Neither Moses nor the ark moved from the camp nor did God and the cloud accompany them. The people were acting entirely apart from the direction of God. Earlier, God had told them, "To morrow turn you, and get you into the wilderness by the way of the Red sea" (v. 25). They were then driven back into the wilderness toward the Red Sea from which they had come.

The first two years of their wilderness experience were a necessary discipline for the people, even though it was probably a longer time than was actually needed for them to cover the distance. But they learned slowly, and we see that after two years they still had not learned to actually take God at His word. As a result of their unbelief and refusal to enter the land, they spent 38 more years in the desert, wandering here and there.

Even though they were God's chosen people, they had been disapproved for their failure to believe God at this crucial time. Salvation was not the issue at stake; rather, going on to maturity with the Lord was involved. But because they refused to believe the word of the Lord, they were severely judged. God refused to go with them against the Canaanites, and He let them be driven back. However, because of the grace and mercy of the Lord, He returned with them to the wilderness for 38 more years. Every day of this time God provided manna and water as well as the shelter of the cloud by day and the light of the pillar of fire by night. The Apostle Paul later spoke of God's longsuffering when he said, "For a period of about forty years He put up with them in the wilderness" (Acts 13:18, NASB).

The people deserved to be in the wilderness alone, without God's sustaining grace, but in His longsuffering He was with them during the entire time. God had made an unconditional promise to Abraham, and not even the unbelief of the people could thwart His presence or His provision for the nation. Although the Israelites had been faithless, God remained faithful to His word. This is a reminder of the New Testament truth: "If we believe not, yet he abideth faithful: he cannot deny himself" (II Tim. 2:13).

The mercy of the Lord to Israel is also indicated by the fact that, even though the older generation had refused to enter the land, God still spoke to the nation about eventually entering it. Numbers 15 begins with the words "And the Lord spake unto Moses, saying, Speak unto the children of Israel, and say unto them, When ye be come into the land of your habitations, which I give unto you" (vv. 1,2).

Thus we see that God did not allow the younger generation to forget about eventually going into the land. God then passed on to the Israelites through Moses the instructions they would need concerning offerings when they entered the land. How ironic that, although the older generation feared to enter the land because of their young ones, only the young ones were able to enter. There is a solemn lesson here for believers today. Although we are to be concerned about our children and grandchildren, we must guard against thinking that even the Lord cannot take care of them and that the younger generation is hopeless. God is still on the throne, and He never forsakes His own. God is not dead; He is able to fulfill His will and purposes.

New Testament Applications

The New Testament refers to these Old Testament incidents in reminding believers not to be guilty of the same faults. Believers are told not to "grumble, as some of them did, and were destroyed by the destroyer. Now these things happened to them as an example, and they were written for our instruction, upon whom the ends of the ages have come" (I Cor. 10:10,11, NASB).

The Book of Hebrews also draws on these Old Testament incidents as warnings to believers. Christians are told: "And with whom was He angry for forty years? Was it not with those who sinned, whose bodies fell in the wilderness? And to whom did He swear that they should not enter His rest, but to those who were disobedient? And so we see that they were not able to enter because of unbelief" (3:17-19, NASB).

Hebrews 4 continues: "Therefore, let us fear lest, while a promise remains of entering His rest, any one of you should seem to have come short of it" (v. 1, NASB). The passage goes on to tell of the lack of faith in God that the Israelites had. Verse 9 contains the application to believers today: "There remaineth therefore a rest to the people of God. For he that is entered into his rest, he also hath ceased from his own works, as God did from his. Let us labour [be diligent] therefore to enter into that rest, lest any man fall after the same example of unbelief" (vv. 9-11).

The "rest" mentioned in this passage is a reference to Christian maturity. It is a rest that results from taking God at His word and applying it to daily life. It is not the rest of heaven or the rest of death but the rest of a position of maturity in Christ Jesus. As indicated in Hebrews 4, this relationship is entered by faith. It is a relationship in which a Christian trusts, or relies on, the Lord Jesus Christ for all of his needs. The mature believer has rest from fear, rest from worry, rest from frustrations and rest from all of the horrible, diabolical side effects that result from fear, worry and frustration.

Many Christians are living far beneath the privileges they have in Christ. As a result their lives are full of worry, fear and guilt, and many even lack the assurance of their salvation. Just as the Israelites were afraid of obstacles when they refused to enter the land, the believer who refuses to enter into a mature relationship with the Lord fears many things in his life. But by active faith, it is possible for a believer to enter into this mature relationship in which he has complete confidence (rest) in Christ.

This active faith is mentioned in Philippians 2:12,13: "Work out your own salvation with fear and trembling. For it is God which worketh in you both to will and to do of his good pleasure." Notice carefully that these verses do not say to work "for" your salvation but to work "out" your salvation. This portion of God's Word is addressed to those who already know Jesus Christ as Saviour—salvation is already in them, but they need to work it out, or express it.

Notice that, according to verse 13, God does two things in the life of a believer. God works in the believer "both to will and to do of his good pleasure." God not only does the work in and through the believer, but He even gives him the desire, or will, to want to magnify Christ in all that he does.

God does not override the personality of the believer in what He does. The Christian must cooperate with God in order for the work of God to be produced in and through his life. Just as an automobile's power steering and power brakes do not work by themselves but must first be activated, so the believer must activate the power of God in his life through faith. The confidence (faith) that a believer has in God activates God to work in and through him. This faith, or trust, relationship is the abundant life spoken of by Christ Himself, recorded in John 10:10. This abundant life is available by faith, for as the believer cooperates with God, he will discover the work of God being accomplished in his life.

It is a shame that many Christians are satisfied with only salvation, or deliverance from condemnation, but ignore and reject the need to go on to a mature relationship with the Lord. Remember Kadesh-barnea. Because the Israelites refused to go on at the place of decision, the result was 38 years of fruitless wandering in the desert. Those years were void of significant accomplishment; the nation was simply marking time until the older generation died off.

A Transition Period

The 38 years of wandering in the wilderness served as a transition period in the history of the Israelites, and it was significant in three ways. First, they neither advanced nor retreated geographically—they simply wandered aimlessly in the wilderness. When the judgment was over 38 years later, they returned to Kadesh-barnea, from which the younger generation moved on toward the land. What happened to Israel then is true of a lot of believers today. They are wandering aimlessly in the Christian life, having no sense of direction and not accomplishing anything significant for the Lord.

Many churches are this way; they go through a routine week after week but do little that is really worthwhile for the Lord. Weak believers and weak churches are only marking time; they are not really moving in a definite direction toward any particular goal.

Second, the population of the nation of Israel was significantly affected during their years of wandering in the wilderness. A generation of over 600,000 warriors died and was buried in the wilderness. Moses referred to this later, saying that the Lord spoke to him "when all the men of war were consumed and dead from among the people" (Deut. 2:16). Actually, all of the older generation, except Joshua and Caleb, died off before the nation was allowed to enter the land. The graves in the wilderness were a daily reminder of God's judgment.

Although there were many deaths in the wilderness, there were also many births as the younger generation grew to adulthood and had children. Thus, the total population was somewhat stabilized, even though so many were dying off.

Third, spiritually, a new hope was born for Israel. The original covenant that God made with Abraham was reaffirmed. Preparations were made at the end of the 38 years to enter the land. Although so many had died off, key leaders were still left to minister to the people—Moses, Aaron, Joshua and Caleb. The earlier promises of the covenant were reaffirmed to Moses when God said, "Behold, I have set the land before you: go in and possess the land which the Lord sware unto your fathers, Abraham, Isaac, and

Jacob, to give unto them and to their seed after them" (Deut. 1:8).

After the years of wandering in the wilderness, God commanded Moses to rise up and begin to march toward the land with the younger generation. But what a sad time it was in Israel's history when so many people lost their lives in the wilderness because of their refusal to take God at His word and to enter the land.

An Example for Believers

As we have stated, Israel's experience serves as a warning to all of us today who know Jesus Christ as personal Saviour. In a sense, every believer comes to a Kadesh-barnea in his life. This is the place of special decision; it is a fork in the road in his Christian life, and he must decide which direction he will go. If he goes on to spiritual maturity, there is eternal potential for his well-being, but if he refuses to go on to spiritual maturity, there will be aimless wandering, just as the Israelites experienced.

Each unsaved individual must make a decision when he is faced with the sin issue and with salvation, which is in Jesus Christ. Each person must decide whether he will reject what Christ has accomplished for him on the cross and continue going his own way or whether he will admit his sinfulness and trust Jesus Christ as his personal Saviour. Those who realize their need and place their faith in Christ as Saviour receive forgiveness of sins and eternal life. What decision have you made in this regard? Are you still trusting yourself and what you can do, or are you trusting Jesus Christ and what He has done for you?

If you have received Christ as your Saviour, your concern should be to glorify Him in every aspect of life and to have an ever-deepening relationship with Him. Each believer comes to a piace of decision, or a Kadesh-barnea, concerning the maturing process in his life. He must decide whether he will go on with the Lord and trust Him completely for every aspect of life or whether he will be content with just being delivered from condemnation.

This place of decision for the believer has a road that leads to victory and usefulness, but it also has a road that leads to despair, disapproval and uselessness. To choose the wrong road is to decide in favor of fear, worry and frustration. Someone has said, "Decisions are the hinges on which the doors of destiny turn." This is not only true of individual believers; it is also true of local churches. Individuals and churches can become stagnant unless they make decisions that lead them on in the way of victory and usefulness.

Just as God had to set aside one entire generation of Israelites before He could bring the nation into the land, there are no doubt instances when God has had to set aside an entire generation in a local church while He waited for another generation to grow to maturity and go on to victory. As Proverbs 29:18 says, "Where there is no vision, the people perish."

The message for the believer today is found in Hebrews 6:1: "Let us go on unto perfection." As has been mentioned, the word translated "perfection" actually means "maturity." When a believer comes to a fork in the road in his spiritual life, it is important that he make the decision that leads him on to maturity. Believers are not to stagnate or go back spiritually as Israel did, wandering aimlessly in the wilderness and wanting to go back to Egypt.

No matter how discouraged we may be with the way our Christian life has been in the past, we cannot go back and start over. Therefore, the only thing to do is to go on from where we are at this point. The Apostle Paul emphasized that Jesus Christ is the foundation in the believer's life (I Cor. 3:11). The need is to continue building on that foundation, not to try laying another foundation (see v. 12).

A believer who is in the wilderness of self is useless to God. The individual may go through the motions of the Christian life, but he does not really magnify God in his life. So also, a local church that is constantly divided over petty issues evidences that it is still in the wilderness of self and is not accomplishing anything significant for God.

A believer's progress from the time of salvation to spiritual maturity parallels the experience of Israel during the journey from Egypt to Canaan. The nation was delivered from Egypt by blood, just as an individual is delivered from condemnation by the shed blood of Christ. Deliverance from

Egypt is comparable to the individual's being delivered from sin and damnation.

Great Salvation

The individual who trusts Christ as Saviour possesses a great salvation. This salvation is far more than just deliverance from condemnation. Hebrews 2:3 asks, "How shall we escape, if we neglect so great salvation?" The salvation referred to is a salvation that leads to spiritual maturity. It is wonderful that sin has been atoned for, but in addition to that, Satan's power has been broken as far as the believer is concerned (see v. 14). At the time of salvation God provides all that the individual needs for eternal life and godliness (II Pet. 1:3,4). All of this is available to those who become the sons of God by receiving Jesus Christ as personal Saviour (John 1:12).

By believing in Christ, a person comes into possession of salvation, and then the person's need is to work out—by continuous faith—that salvation in and through his life (see Phil. 2:12,13). Nothing is lacking in what God has provided for us, for we "are complete in him" (Col. 2:10).

God also gives the believer a wonderful position in Christ in the heavenlies. Ephesians 2:6 says God "hath raised us up together, and made us sit together in heavenly places in Christ Jesus." This position in Christ reveals that the believer is positionally in the place of the victor because Christ is victorious over all. The Lord Jesus Christ has given us all the weapons necessary for the spiritual warfare we face. The Bible says, "For though we walk in the flesh, we do not war after the flesh: (for the weapons of our warfare are not carnal, but mighty through God to the pulling down of strong holds;) casting down imaginations, and every high thing that exalteth itself against the knowledge of God, and bringing into captivity every thought to the obedience of Christ" (II Cor. 10:3-5).

God has given the believer all he needs for spiritual victory. But the believer must choose whether or not he will go on to the place of spiritual victory and maturity, which involves a continuous application of faith in the indwelling Christ (see Gal. 2:20). This is why Hebrews 6:1 encourages believers to go on, and verse 3 says, "And this will we do, if God permit." Have you wondered what is meant by the words "if God permit"? I believe this refers to the type of experience Israel had at Kadesh-barnea. God wanted them to go on into the land, but they refused because of their unbelief. When God announced the judgment that would come on them, they changed their minds and wanted to go into the land, but God would not permit it. They had experienced so many spiritual blessings and had witnessed the magnificent powers of God, but even with such knowledge they had refused to go on to victory when God gave them the opportunity.

So remember Israel's situation as you consider decisions you must make in your spiritual life. Although they had been away from Egypt for two years and had seen the display of God's power, they sinned against better knowledge. They looked at themselves, and they looked at the giants, but they refused to look at God. As a result, God had to set them on the shelf, and the nation spent the next 38 years in fruitless activity because the people refused to believe God. May our lives always be characterized by active belief, which results in victorious (mature) Christian living.

Chapter 9

Moses Sins Under Pressure

Because of the unbelief which the Israelites displayed at Kadesh-barnea, the next 38 years were spent in aimless wandering while the older generation died. All, that is, except Joshua and Caleb.

Numbers 20 reveals that Miriam died at Kadesh-barnea, but the leadership of the nation was still in the hands of Moses and Aaron. Throughout Moses' life he had been characterized by faithfulness and selflessness, but a situation developed that caused his life to end in a minor key. He was presented with a situation, and under the pressure of it he did not glorify the Lord. As a result he was not able to enter the Promised Land. At first it might seem that this was a severe penalty for what one might consider a small matter. However, a careful analysis of this incident shows that it was not such a small matter after all.

No Water

After the years of wandering in the wilderness, the Israelites returned to Kadesh-barnea, where Miriam died (Num. 20:1). There was no water for the people to drink, so they sided against Moses and Aaron and said, "Would God that we had died when our brethren died before the Lord! And why have ye brought up the congregation of the Lord into this wilderness, that we and our cattle should die there? And wherefore have ye made us to come up out of Egypt, to bring us in unto this evil place? It is no place of seed, or of figs, or of vines, or of pomegranates; neither is there any water to drink" (vv. 3-5).

126

Notice what the complaint of the people really was. They had seen the solemn judgment God had meted out on their parents and grandparents over a period of 38 years. Perhaps some of the older generation were still living at this time, but most of them had died in the wilderness and had been buried by the younger ones. The younger generation knew very well why God had judged Israel—because of unbelief.

The same Israelites who grumbled because of the lack of water had seen the fatherliness of God toward them through Moses, their aged leader. God had provided all they needed—even out in the desert during the 38 years of aimless wandering. But although they had experienced the provisions of their miracle-working God, they vehemently took issue with Moses and ultimately with God as they faced a lack of water. They charged Moses with having brought them to "this evil place" (v. 5). They were not in the land of Canaan yet, but apparently they referred to it in their grumbling and even called God's Promised Land an "evil place."

It had been 40 years since the Israelites had left the land of Egypt, and they had experienced God's constant supply during all those 40 years. But their children insulted God by questioning His goodness and wisdom. What a wonder that God did not strike them dead right there!

Notice how Moses and Aaron responded—they "went from the presence of the assembly unto the door of the tabernacle of the congregation, and they fell upon their faces: and the glory of the Lord appeared unto them" (v. 6). What a great God Moses and Aaron had! He was a God of judgment because He was a righteous God, but He was also a God of compassion, and He revealed Himself to them.

God told Moses what to do: "Take the rod, and gather thou the assembly together, thou, and Aaron thy brother, and speak ye unto the rock before their eyes; and it shall give forth his water, and thou shalt bring forth to them water out of the rock: so thou shalt give the congregation and their beasts drink" (v. 8).

Observe the threefold instructions: (1) "Take the rod"; (2) "gather thou the assembly together"; (3) "speak ye unto the rock before their eyes."

Two Rods and Two Rocks

The rod that Moses took was a distinctive rod. Numbers 20:9 says, "And Moses took the rod from before the Lord, as he commanded him." The indication is that this was a different rod than the one commonly used by Moses.

Nearly 40 years had passed since Moses had used his rod to deliver the Israelites from Egypt. He also used his own rod when he struck the rock in Horeb to bring forth water, as recorded in Exodus 17. At that time God told Moses, "Go on before the people, and take with thee of the elders of Israel; and thy rod, wherewith thou smotest the river, take in thine hand, and go. Behold, I will stand before thee there upon the rock in Horeb; and thou shalt smite the rock, and there shall come water out of it, that the people may drink" (vv. 5,6). Moses did as the Lord instructed, and the people had water.

The rock mentioned in Exodus 17 foreshadowed Christ on the cross because there He was smitten. However, the rock of Numbers 20 foreshadowed the ascended Christ, who now intercedes as a high priest for believers. The significant difference in the rocks of Exodus 17 and Numbers 20 is also indicated in that a different word for "rock" is used in these two passages. Although both rocks speak of Christ, God was endeavoring to communicate two different things to us concerning the Person of Christ.

In Exodus 17 the rock was smitten, just as Christ was "smitten of God" (Isa. 53:4) and was "bruised for our iniquities" (v. 5). The rock of Numbers 20 foreshadowed Christ in the heavens, as referred to in Hebrews 9:24: "For Christ is not entered into the holy places made with hands, which are the figures of the true; but into heaven itself, now to appear in the presence of God for us." Hebrews 7:25 tells what Christ is doing in heaven for us: "Wherefore he is able also to save them to the uttermost that come unto God by him, seeing he ever liveth to make intercession for them." Because Christ ever lives, He has an "unchangeable priesthood" (v. 24). So the rock of Numbers 20 refers to this priestly work of Christ after His resurrection, ascension and exaltation at the right hand of the Father.

Not only was there a difference between the two rocks, but there was also a difference between the two rods. As mentioned previously, God told Moses to "take the rod" (Num. 20:8), and "Moses took the rod from before the Lord" (v. 9). During the other incident where water was needed (Ex. 17), God told Moses, "Take . . . thy rod, wherewith thou smotest the river, take in thine hand, and go. Behold, I will stand before thee there upon the rock in Horeb; and thou shalt smite the rock, and there shall come water out of it, that the people may drink" (vv. 5,6). That rod was clearly identified as the one which Moses used at the Red Sea. However, the rod of Numbers 20 is the one Moses took "from before the Lord" (v. 9).

The background concerning this rod that Moses took from before the Lord is given in Numbers 17. After Korah and his followers questioned the authority of Moses and Aaron over the Israelites, God told Moses to take a rod from each of the 12 tribes and to write their names on them. He was also to write the name of Aaron on the rod of Levi. Moses was instructed to lay the rods in the tabernacle, and God said, "It shall come to pass, that the man's rod, whom I shall choose, shall blossom: and I will make to cease from me the murmurings of the children of Israel, whereby they murmur against you" (v. 5). On the next day "the rod of Aaron for the house of Levi was budded, and brought forth buds, and bloomed blossoms, and yielded almonds" (v. 8).

Then note what the Lord instructed Moses: "Bring Aaron's rod again before the testimony, to be kept for a token against the rebels; and thou shalt quite take away their murmurings from me, that they die not" (v. 10). So the rod was placed in the ark of the covenant as a testimony to Israel of God's choice of Moses and Aaron as the leaders of the nation.

Hebrews 9:4 says that the ark of the covenant contained "the golden pot that had manna, and Aaron's rod that budded, and the tables of the covenant." Aaron's rod was a priestly rod, in contrast to the rod of Moses, which was a rod of judgment.

Foreshadowings of Christ

In this second incident where water was needed, Moses was not to use the rod of judgment but the priestly rod to bring forth water. Another distinction between the two incidents is that in Exodus 17 Moses went alone with the rod of judgment, whereas in Numbers 20 he was instructed to go with Aaron and to speak to the rock (v. 8). Aaron was the high priest, so this adds significance to the occasion and further emphasizes the priestly aspect of the rock as it foreshadowed the intercessory work of the Lord Jesus Christ.

At the incident of Exodus 17, which took place right after the Israelites had come out of Egypt, the emphasis was judgment; at the incident of Numbers 20, which took place just prior to their entering the land, the emphasis was on priestly work. Israel had been redeemed from Egypt by blood, just as redemption is provided for all through the shed blood of Jesus Christ. So judgment was the key element associated with the rock in Exodus 17.

Just prior to entering the land, however, the great need of Israel was to rely on God for everything. Thus, the rock of Numbers 20 represented Christ, the High Priest, at the right hand of the Father, who only needs to be spoken to. There was to be no striking of the rock, inasmuch as it prefigured Christ, who had already been smitten. Since His death was sufficient to pay the penalty for all sin, there was no need for Him to be smitten again. That the rock of Numbers 20 foreshadowed the Lord Jesus Christ is evident from I Corinthians 10:4: "They drank of that spiritual Rock that followed them: and that Rock was Christ."

The Scriptures make it clear that Christ died for sin once and for all. Romans 6:9,10 says, "Knowing that Christ being raised from the dead dieth no more; death hath no more dominion over him. For in that he died, he died unto sin once: but in that he liveth, he liveth unto God."

Concerning Christ, the Book of Hebrews says, "Nor yet that he should offer himself often, as the high priest entereth into the holy place every year with blood of others; for then must he often have suffered since the foundation of the world: but now once in the end of the world [ages] hath he appeared to put away sin by the sacrifice of himself. . . . So Christ was once offered to bear the sins of many; and unto them that look for him shall he appear the second time without sin unto salvation" (9:25,26,28). The Book of

Hebrews also states, "We are sanctified through the offering of the body of Jesus Christ once for all. . . . For by one offering he hath perfected for ever them that are sanctified" (10:10,14). Death came to Christ only once; now He ever lives to make intercession (7:25).

In the incident of Numbers 20 the rock foreshadowed the exalted Christ, and that is why it needed only to be spoken to. It is so important that this distinction between the smitten Christ and the exalted Christ as He is foreshadowed in the two rocks be maintained.

Since the Lord Jesus Christ has been judged on the cross by having all of the sins of the world placed on Him, those of us who have received Him as Saviour need now to speak to Him for our needs. And just as His death was effective for all sin, His intercessory work is effective for all of our needs.

Hebrews 10:19-23 reveals the boldness believers can have in approaching the throne of grace. This significant passage says, "Having therefore, brethren, boldness to enter into the holiest by the blood of Jesus, by a new and living way, which he hath consecrated for us, through the veil, that is to say, his flesh; and having an high priest over the house of God; let us draw near with a true heart in full assurance of faith, having our hearts sprinkled from an evil conscience, and our bodies washed with pure water. Let us hold fast the profession of our faith without wavering; (for he is faithful that promised)."

The injunction to hold fast to the profession of our faith is similar to the earlier exhortation in Hebrews: "Let us go on unto perfection [maturity]" (6:1). To go back (v. 6) would be to crucify Christ again.

Just as Christ was smitten only once, the Holy Spirit is given to believers only once. Thereafter they simply come to Him and drink to the full. This is the analogy used by Christ Himself when He said, "If any man thirst, let him come unto me, and drink. He that believeth on me, as the scripture hath said, out of his belly shall flow rivers of living water. (But this spake he of the Spirit, which they that believe on him should receive: for the Holy Ghost was not yet given; because that Jesus was not yet glorified.)" (John 7:37-39).

Moses Strikes the Rock

In spite of the fact that God had told him to take the rod and speak to the rock, Moses momentarily lost his self-control and lashed out at the Israelites. He said, "Hear now, ye rebels; must we fetch you water out of this rock?" (Num. 20:10).

In his anger, instead of speaking to the rock as God had instructed, "Moses lifted up his hand, and with his rod he smote the rock twice" (v. 11). In a way this was the most crucial moment in the life of Moses, and it holds some serious lessons for us today. In one brief, impulsive act, this great man of God forfeited his opportunity to lead the people of Israel into the Promised Land. He had led them for nearly 40 years—from Egypt to the edge of Canaan—but God refused to let him go into the land because of his disobedience at this point.

After Moses struck the rock twice, the Lord told him and Aaron, "Because ye believed me not, to sanctify me in the eyes of the children of Israel, therefore ye shall not bring this congregation into the land which I have given them" (v. 12).

We might excuse Moses for hitting the rock instead of speaking to it, but his actions were significant because of what the rock foreshadowed. Even though we might overlook something and think it was only a slight sin, let us not forget that God looks at matters differently than we do. Isaiah 55:8,9 says, "For my thoughts are not your thoughts, neither are your ways my ways, saith the Lord. For as the heavens are higher than the earth, so are my ways higher than your ways, and my thoughts than your thoughts."

We cannot tell God what to do nor can we counsel Him; He has all wisdom and is absolutely righteous in all His acts. The Apostle Paul realized this, and he exclaimed, "How fathomless the depths of God's resources, wisdom, and knowledge! How unsearchable His decisions, and how mysterious His methods! For who has ever understood the thoughts of the Lord, or has ever been His adviser? Or who has ever advanced God anything to have Him pay him back? For from Him everything comes, through Him everything lives, and for Him everything exists. Glory to Him forever!" (Rom. 11:33-36, Williams).

Some Christians today think that we should not emphasize the sins of a person like Moses. It is true that the sins of a person should not be overemphasized in contrast to his acts that glorify the Lord; however, it is what a person does with his sin that makes him great in the eyes of God. All are sinners, but not all are willing to face that fact and cry out to God for forgiveness. As I John 1:9 indicates, those who confess their sins are forgiven by God, but it takes great strength of character to admit sin and confess it to the Lord. Great is the person who comes clean before God concerning his sin.

In the Bible God does not present a false concept of those He used mightily. Whether it was David or Moses or someone else, God reveals the sin they were guilty of but also reveals how they claimed forgiveness and became great men with Him. In spite of the fact that David committed terrible sins, he was known as a man after the heart of God (I Sam. 13:14). He came clean before the Lord concerning his sin, and Psalm 51 records his confession.

Consequences of Moses' Sin

Even though God forgives sin, there are often consequences that must be suffered in this life. Such was the case with Moses. He was the greatest prophet who ever lived other than Christ (see Deut. 34:10), but because of this sin he was not able to enter the land of Canaan. God forgave him of the sin, but there were still consequences to be suffered.

Moses and Aaron suffered the consequences because they misrepresented Christ in this second incident of bringing water from the rock. Since this second rock foreshadowed Christ in His high-priestly work as one who only needs to be spoken to, they did not exalt Him when they struck the rock—and especially when they struck it twice. Thus, Moses and Aaron had to reap the consequences of their disobedience. The reason the consequences were so severe was that much more was involved than is seen on the surface of this passage of scripture.

Because of Moses' and Aaron's unbelief God was not sanctified in the eyes of the people; it was as if they were putting Christ to an open shame the second time. Numbers

20 indicates that God brings chastisement on those who, by their actions, imply that Christ can be put to open shame again.

The sobering lesson from this incident concerning Moses and Aaron is that God deals more severely with leaders, especially when their public action brings dishonor to His glory. God told them, "Because ye believed me not, to sanctify me in the eyes of the children of Israel, therefore ye shall not bring this congregation into the land which I have given them" (v. 12). The New Testament refers to leaders' having greater responsibility when it says, "Let not many of you become teachers, my brethren, knowing that as such we shall incur a stricter judgment" (James 3:1, NASB).

But whether you are a leader or not, it is important that you come clean before God concerning sin if you know Jesus Christ as your Saviour. The Apostle John told believers, "My little children, these things write I unto you, that ye sin not. And if any man sin, we have an advocate with the Father, Jesus Christ the righteous [one]" (I John 2:1). Jesus Christ pleads the case of those who have trusted Him as personal Saviour. And because His shed blood on the cross was effective in paying for all sin, His intercession is effective for all who call on Him. "Let us therefore come boldly unto the throne of grace, that we may obtain mercy, and find grace to help in time of need" (Heb. 4:16).

So although Moses had to suffer as a result of his sin, forgiveness was available because of God's mercy. And out of His grace God also provided for the people of Israel. Even though Moses had struck the rock twice instead of speaking to it, God manifested His grace to the people in that He supplied the water they needed: "The water came out abundantly, and the congregation drank, and their beasts also" (Num. 20:11).

What a wonderful God we have! His grace produces results even when He is poorly represented. The people did not suffer because of their leader's sin. Man's unbelief does not nullify the power of God. As II Timothy 2:13 says, "If we believe not, yet he abideth faithful: he cannot deny himself."

Even though Moses was told at this time that he would not be able to enter the land because of his act of unbelief, he later asked the Lord for permission to enter the land. When Moses later reviewed the history of the nation for the Israelites, he told them, "And I besought the Lord at that time, saying, O Lord God, thou hast begun to shew thy servant thy greatness, and thy mighty hand: for what God is there in heaven or in earth, that can do according to thy works, and according to thy might? I pray thee, let me go over, and see the good land that is beyond Jordan, that goodly mountain, and Lebanon. But the Lord was wroth with me for your sakes, and would not hear me: and the Lord said unto me, Let it suffice thee; speak no more unto me of this matter" (Deut. 3:23-26).

So although Moses' sin was forgiven, he had to suffer its consequences by not being allowed to enter the Promised Land. Sin leaves its effect. Galatians 6:7 says, "Whatsoever a man soweth, that shall he also reap." Moses did not lose his salvation because of his sin, but he lost much in the way of reward during his earthly life because he did not accomplish the goal that for years he had his eyes fixed on.

Chapter 10
Great in His Farewell

The last year of Moses' life was as full of work as any other prior to it. The conquest of the land east of Canaan took place during that year. The two Canaanite chiefs, Sihon and Og, were conquered, and the land on the east of the Jordan was designated for two and a half tribes of Israel.

Then followed a series of farewell addresses, which contained Moses' last charges to the people. The Book of Deuteronomy records these addresses, which were full of emotion and stirring appeals. Moses spoke much about the past, revealed his gratitude to God as well as his fear of God, and spoke of the results of self-interest and the danger of sin as the people prepared to enter the land. The farewell messages of Moses revealed how greatly he loved his people, for he poured out his heart to them and was so concerned for their future.

A New Leader

In the last year of Moses' life Joshua was appointed to succeed him as Israel's leader. In Moses' concern for the people, he asked God, "Let the Lord, the God of the spirits of all flesh, set a man over the congregation, which may go out before them, and which may go in before them, and which may lead them out, and which may bring them in; that the congregation of the Lord be not as sheep which have no shepherd" (Num. 27:16,17).

Notice that Moses was concerned that the Israelites not be "as sheep which have no shepherd." The Lord Jesus Christ used a similar analogy in John 10 when He revealed Himself as "the good shepherd" (v. 14).

Note the five qualifications that Moses stipulated for the future leader. Numbers 27:17 lists them. He was to be a man who: (1) "may go out before them"—one who would lead them; (2) one who "may go in before them"—one who could intercede in behalf of the people; (3) one who "may lead them out"—one who would be an able leader in warfare; (4) one who "may bring them in"—one who would lead them into the land; (5) one who would give proper leadership so that "the congregation of the Lord be not as sheep which have no shepherd." These are significant qualifications which Moses realized would be needed by the one who would successfully lead that great people.

This passage also reveals the principle that those in places of responsibility should be careful to establish proper leadership under them. This is a principle we have sought to carry out at Back to the Bible. I remember clearly that we sought for God's man to head up the Missions Department about 25 years ago. We waited for over two years for God's man, but it was well worth the wait. G. Christian Weiss has served the Lord and Back to the Bible ably since he was sent to us by God. When we needed another assistant, we waited on God for His choice. That choice was Ord Morrow, who joined us in 1959. We know that we must wait on God so that the leadership is distinctly His choice, not just ours.

After Moses made known his request for a leader, the Lord said to him, "Take thee Joshua the son of Nun, a man in whom is the spirit, and lay thine hand upon him; and set him before Eleazar the priest, and before all the congregation; and give him a charge in their sight. And thou shalt put some of thine honour upon him, that all the congregation of the children of Israel may be obedient. And he shall stand before Eleazar the priest, who shall ask counsel for him after the judgment of Urim before the Lord: at his word shall they go out, and at his word they shall come in, both he, and all the children of Israel with him, even all the congregation" (vv. 18-21).

Joshua was the individual who was to succeed Moses, the greatest prophet who ever lived other than Christ (see Deut.

34:10). Joshua was one of the spies who had brought back a good report of the land and had encouraged the people to believe God and take the land (see Num. 14:6-9). As he was chosen as Moses' successor, he was specifically described as being "a man in whom is the spirit" (27:18). Although he possessed the Spirit, Joshua was not to receive his directions directly from the Lord as did Moses. Moses knew the Lord "face to face" (Deut. 34:10), but Joshua was to receive his instructions through Eleazar the priest (Num. 27:21). Moses was not only a prophet, but in a sense he was also a priest, since he received revelation directly from God. Joshua, however, received God's message from the high priest, who in turn received revelation from God. Somehow God communicated with the priest through the Urim and Thummim, and then the priest communicated God's will to Joshua.

After God instructed him concerning Joshua, "Moses did as the Lord commanded him" (v. 22). Moses' life was characterized by obedience. He laid his hands on Joshua and bestowed honor on him. God had said, "Thou shalt put some of thine honour upon him, that all the congregation of the children of Israel may be obedient" (v. 20).

Moses' Birthday Message

Especially significant in the last year of Moses' life was the celebration of his 120th birthday. Moses said to the Israelites, "I am an hundred and twenty years old this day; I can no more go out and come in: also the Lord hath said unto me, Thou shalt not go over this Jordan. The Lord thy God, he will go over before thee, and he will destroy these nations from before thee, and thou shalt possess them: and Joshua, he shall go over before thee, as the Lord hath said" (Deut. 31:2,3).

In his birthday message, Moses gave solemn charges to the Israelites and to Joshua. He charged Israel with the responsibility to go into the land and take it from the nations inhabiting it. Moses told the Israelites, "The Lord shall give them up before your face, that ye may do unto them according unto all the commandments which I have commanded you. Be strong and of a good courage, fear not, nor be afraid of them: for the Lord thy God, he it is that doth go with thee; he will not fail thee, nor forsake thee" (vv. 5,6).

Moses then gave a solemn charge to Joshua: "Be strong and of a good courage: for thou must go with this people unto the land which the Lord hath sworn unto their fathers to give them; and thou shalt cause them to inherit it. And the Lord, he it is that doth go before thee; he will be with thee, he will not fail thee, neither forsake thee: fear not, neither be dismayed" (vv. 7,8).

After Moses had made his solemn charges to Israel and to Joshua, God said to Moses, "Behold, thy days approach that thou must die: call Joshua, and present yourselves in the tabernacle of the congregation, that I may give him a charge" (v. 14). The Lord Himself then appeared "in a pillar of a cloud" (v. 15) and said to Moses, "Behold, thou shalt sleep with thy fathers; and this people will rise up, and go a whoring after the gods of the strangers of the land, whither they go to be among them, and will forsake me, and break my covenant which I have made with them. Then my anger shall be kindled against them in that day, and I will forsake them, and I will hide my face from them, and they shall be devoured, and many evils and troubles shall befall them; so that they will say in that day, Are not these evils come upon us, because our God is not among us?" (vv. 16,17).

So God warned what would happen after the people entered the land; there would be apostasy with its resulting judgment. But to Joshua there was the charge "Be strong and of a good courage: for thou shalt bring the children of Israel into the land which I sware unto them: and I will be with thee" (v. 23).

Moses then delivered a final charge to the Levites. After he had finished writing the Law in a book, he told the Levites, "Take this book of the law, and put it in the side of the ark of the covenant of the Lord your God, that it may be there for a witness against thee. For I know thy rebellion, and thy stiff neck: behold, while I am yet alive with you this day, ye have been rebellious against the Lord; and how much more after my death?" (vv. 26,27).

Moses' Song and Benediction

Moses then called all the leaders together and delivered to them what is commonly known as "The Song of Moses." This song, recorded in Deuteronomy 32, is one of the most sublime compositions on record. It has been called the "Magna Charta of Prophecy."

Moses' song can only be compared to one other song—the song of the Lamb. The song of Moses and the song of the Lamb are both mentioned in Revelation 15:3: "And they sing the song of Moses the servant of God, and the song of the Lamb, saying, Great and marvellous are thy works, Lord God Almighty; just and true are thy ways, thou King of saints."

After Moses had delivered his song to the Israelites, he pronounced a great benediction on them. This benediction is recorded in Deuteronomy 33, which begins with the words "And this is the blessing, wherewith Moses the man of God blessed the children of Israel before his death" (v. 1).

The chapter concludes with these significant words: "There is none like unto the God of Jeshurun, who rideth upon the heaven in thy help, and in his excellency on the sky. The eternal God is thy refuge, and underneath are the everlasting arms: and he shall thrust out the enemy from before thee; and shall say, Destroy them. Israel then shall dwell in safety alone: the fountain of Jacob shall be upon a land of corn and wine; also his heavens shall drop down dew. Happy art thou, O Israel: who is like unto thee, O people saved by the Lord, the shield of thy help, and who is the sword of thy excellency! And thine enemies shall be found liars unto thee; and thou shalt tread upon their high places" (vv. 26-29).

How characteristic it was of Moses to extol the love and care of Almighty God!

Chapter 11

Great in His Death

Moses was not only great in his works, his meekness and his farewell, but he was also great in his death.

We have looked at the inner life of this noble man, and we have seen that all he accomplished was because his heart was fixed on the Lord. His soul's secret abiding place was in God. To Moses, God was his home, his help and his stay. Moses recognized that he was nothing in himself and that everything he accomplished was because of God's indwelling presence. Because Moses relied completely on God, he was greatly used by God in a way no other individual, apart from the Lord Jesus Christ, has been used.

What was accomplished in Moses' life was due to the indwelling Holy Spirit, who fulfilled the work of God in Moses' life. During Old Testament times, the Holy Spirit did not indwell every believer as He does today. The Holy Spirit came upon chosen believers to empower them for service, enabling them to accomplish God's specific work. Since the Day of Pentecost, however, the Holy Spirit has indwelt every believer. The Apostle Paul emphasized this truth when he referred to each believer's body as a temple of the Holy Spirit (I Cor. 6:19). The ministry of the Spirit in Old and New Testament times and today is to work out through the believer that which God has worked in him. This is especially indicated in Philippians 2:12,13, where believers are told: "Work out your own salvation with fear and trembling. For it is God which worketh in you both to will and to do of his good pleasure."

As Moses drew to the close of his life, he was great in his death just as he had been great in his life. At this point a

141

backward look gives perspective to a forward look. He was forbidden to enter the land because he struck the rock instead of speaking to it. This sin was so serious because of what the rock foreshadowed—Christ's intercessory ministry.

Moses' Last Request

Although Moses' life had been lived as a great symphony, it ended in a minor key. In his last request of God, he asked for something that was denied. This is especially significant when one realizes all that Moses had been granted by God as he had interceded in the past. God was on the verge of destroying the Israelites more than once, but Moses had stood in the gap and had successfully interceded for them. The psalmist said, "Therefore he said that he would destroy them, had not Moses his chosen stood before him in the breach, to turn away his wrath, lest he should destroy them" (Ps. 106:23).

The last request of Moses, which was rejected by God, is recorded in Deuteronomy 3:23-27. Moses told the Israelites, "I besought the Lord at that time, saying, O Lord God, thou hast begun to shew thy servant thy greatness, and thy mighty hand: for what God is there in heaven or in earth, that can do according to thy works, and according to thy might? I pray thee, let me go over, and see the good land that is beyond Jordan, that goodly mountain, and Lebanon. But the Lord was wroth with me for your sakes, and would not hear me: and the Lord said unto me, Let it suffice thee; speak no more unto me of this matter. Get thee up into the top of Pisgah, and lift up thine eyes westward, and northward, and southward, and eastward, and behold it with thine eyes: for thou shalt not go over this Jordan."

This denial of Moses' request was especially significant in light of Moses' great intercessions at Mount Sinai and at Kadesh-barnea, as well as for Miriam and Korah.

Moses was greatly disappointed about not being able to enter into the land. He said to the Israelites, "The Lord was wroth with me for your sakes, and would not hear me: and the Lord said unto me, Let it suffice thee; speak no more unto me of this matter" (v. 26).

Moses' sin was forgiven because he had confessed it to God, and he had been restored to full fellowship with God. However, the judicial consequences of his sin remained. This is the principle by which God works even today. Galatians 6:7,8 says, "Be not deceived; God is not mocked: for whatsoever a man soweth, that shall he also reap. For he that soweth to his flesh shall of the flesh reap corruption; but he that soweth to the Spirit shall of the Spirit reap life everlasting." So there are judicial consequences even though the person confesses his sin and is restored to fellowship with God. When sin is confessed, however, the person suffers no eternal consequences because of it.

God told Moses not to ask again for permission to enter the land. Although the Bible tells us to "pray without ceasing" (I Thess. 5:17) and to "ask," "seek" and "knock" (Matt. 7:7), God makes it clear at times that we are not to ask again.

This was true in the Apostle Paul's life. He had a "thorn in the flesh" (II Cor. 12:7) and asked the Lord three times to remove it from him. God's response, however, was "My grace is sufficient for thee: for my strength is made perfect in weakness" (v. 9). God made it clear to Paul that the thorn was to keep him from becoming too exalted because of the revelation he had received from God.

Moses Confesses

Although Moses' last request was not answered, his great character was seen in that he confessed his sin before all of the Israelites. He "besought the Lord at that time" (Deut. 3:23), but his request was denied. The Lord told him to go to the top of Pisgah, where he would see the Promised Land, but he would not be able to enter it (v. 27).

When God denied his request, Moses did not continue to beg God to let him enter the land. Just as Moses had accepted God's word many other times in his life, he accepted this denial, even though it was not what he preferred to hear.

Because of Moses' nature, it is safe to assume that he did not make only a general confession about his sin of striking the rock instead of speaking to it. While no verse says it in so many words, Moses was the type who faced sin specifically.

We need to follow Moses' example—we need to face sin squarely and not minimize or explain it away. There are those who say, "Lord, if I have sinned, please forgive." It is true that sometimes we do not know where or how we might have sinned, but at those times we should be like the psalmist and pray, "Search me, O God, and know my heart: try me, and know my thoughts: and see if there be any wicked way in me, and lead me in the way everlasting" (Ps. 139:23,24).

When God puts His finger on the sin we have committed, it is then our responsibility to agree with God concerning it—this is actually what "confess" means. When we agree with God that it is sin, then we can claim the promise of God that He forgives when we confess (I John 1:9).

We are often slow to humble ourselves as Moses did and readily admit a great sin. A private sin needs to be confessed only to God because only He and the individual know about it. A public sin, however, needs to be confessed publicly, in addition to being confessed to God. The confession should be as extensive as the sin, no less and no more.

Some do not believe that even public sin should be confessed publicly because, they say, it lowers one in the eyes of the people. But just the opposite is true. When the people know an individual has sinned, he will never have a good testimony before them again until he admits his sin.

Moses' admission of his sin elevated him in the estimation of the people because he had come clean with them as he had with God concerning his sin. When God put His finger on the sin in Moses' life, Moses readily admitted it to God and to the people.

Moses' meekness at this point in his life is seen in that he showed no trace of jealousy or envy when his successor was announced. The Lord told Moses, "But charge Joshua, and encourage him, and strengthen him: for he shall go over before this people, and he shall cause them to inherit the land which thou shalt see" (Deut. 3:28).

Moses did something that is extremely difficult to do. With beautiful self-emptiness he stepped down from his elevated position, threw his mantle over the shoulders of his successor and encouraged him to discharge with holy fidelity the duties of that high office from which he had to resign.

Moses publicly stepped down from his position and put

his full approval on Joshua as God had asked him to do. "Moses called unto Joshua, and said unto him in the sight of all Israel, Be strong and of a good courage: for thou must go with this people unto the land which the Lord hath sworn unto their fathers to give them; and thou shalt cause them to inherit it. And the Lord, he it is that doth go before thee; he will be with thee, he will not fail thee, neither forsake thee: fear not, neither be dismayed" (31:7,8).

Even in Moses' dying moments, he humbled himself under the mighty hand of God. He accepted the discipline imposed on him by God, and he did not murmur at the refusal of his request. Because of this humble attitude, Moses was later exalted by God. Moses was great in his life, but he was just as great in his dying moments.

Moses Views the Land

Although God's discipline kept Moses out of Canaan, God's grace conducted him to Pisgah's top, where, in the Lord's company, he was permitted to view the land. Actually, three names are used in reference to the place from which Moses viewed the Promised Land—Pisgah, Nebo and Abarim. This may seem confusing, but the different names refer to different parts of the same general location. Mount Nebo was the head, or summit, of Mount Pisgah, which was a portion of the mountain range called Abarim.

"The Lord spake unto Moses that selfsame day, saying, Get thee up into this mountain Abarim, unto mount Nebo, which is in the land of Moab, that is over against Jericho; and behold the land of Canaan, which I give unto the children of Israel for a possession" (Deut. 32:48,49). The day referred to by the words "selfsame day" (v. 48) was the day of Moses' 120th birthday (see 31:2). What an unusual birthday celebration! Although Moses was not allowed to enter the Promised Land, he was allowed to see it as no other man ever saw it.

Deuteronomy 34:1-3 records the breathtaking view of the land that Moses had. It was possibly the greatest emotional experience in his lifetime. These verses say, "And Moses went up from the plains of Moab unto the mountain of Nebo, to the top of Pisgah, that is over against Jericho.

And the Lord shewed him all the land of Gilead, unto Dan, and all Naphtali, and the land of Ephraim, and Manasseh, and all the land of Judah, unto the utmost sea, and the south, and the plain of the valley of Jericho, the city of palm trees, unto Zoar."

God must have given Moses a special ability to see and caused the sky to be clear that day so Moses could view the land. After showing Moses the land, God said to him, "This is the land which I sware unto Abraham, unto Isaac, and unto Jacob, saying, I will give it unto thy seed: I have caused thee to see it with thine eyes, but thou shalt not go over thither" (v. 4).

The entire passage of Deuteronomy 32:48—34:4 gives a complete description of those events preceding Moses' death. Here we see the typically selfless heart of Moses. There was not a word of self-pity or mourning; there was not even an expression of his great excitement about having God show him all the lands of Israel's inheritance.

Even at the mature age of 120—after faithfully leading his people through agonizing years of tribulation—he was still in prime physical condition: "His eye was not dim, nor his natural force abated" (34:7). And, as was typical of Moses, he obeyed his Master to the end. A phrase that characterized the life of Moses was "Moses did as the Lord commanded him" (Num. 27:22).

Moses' Triumph in Death

God's last command to Moses was that he was to go to the mountaintop and die there, after having viewed the land. God told Moses, "Get thee up into this mountain Abarim, unto mount Nebo, which is in the land of Moab, that is over against Jericho; and behold the land of Canaan, which I give unto the children of Israel for a possession: and die in the mount whither thou goest up, and be gathered unto thy people; as Aaron thy brother died in mount Hor, and was gathered unto his people" (Deut. 32:49,50).

Moses was to go alone. This was his last step of obedience, and even this demonstrates the aloneness of Moses.

Aloneness is the price that often has to be paid for great leadership. But aloneness must not be confused with loneliness. The Christian leader realizes that, even though he must stand alone at times, God stands with him, so there is no loneliness. God's most effective work in the heart of an individual is often accomplished when that person is alone.

Alone Moses worked, suffered, met God and legislated for his people. But never was this aloneness as apparent as when he was unattended—even by Joshua, his ever-faithful servant—as he walked up Mount Nebo to die. Alone he climbed the craggy steep. Alone he gazed on the landscape before him. And alone he lay down to die. At the moment of death he was absolutely alone—no one in Israel stood by him.

Yet God was with Moses. In a sense, God was Moses' undertaker, and the angels were his pallbearers. God was also the custodian of the grave, for no one knew where Moses was buried.

No tombstone was placed on Moses' grave—no monument to indicate the remains of this great man of God. The epitaph of Moses was not on a tombstone but was recorded in God's eternal Word, written there by the Holy Spirit Himself. No finer epitaph of Moses could be recorded than what is stated in Deuteronomy 34:10-12: "And there arose not a prophet since in Israel like unto Moses, whom the Lord knew face to face, in all the signs and the wonders, which the Lord sent him to do in the land of Egypt to Pharaoh, and to all his servants, and to all his land, and in all that mighty hand, and in all the great terror which Moses shewed in the sight of all Israel." This is God's epitaph for this great man.

Hebrews 11:27 could also be an epitaph of Moses' life: "He endured, as seeing him who is invisible." What a eulogy! One reads of what many accomplished in the temporal and visible realm, but this man was ruled by the invisible. What a man of faith!

The Book of Jude reveals that there was a battle for the body of Moses after his death. Verse 9 says, "Yet Michael the archangel, when contending with the devil he disputed about the body of Moses, durst not bring against him a railing accusation, but said, The Lord rebuke thee." There is nothing to indicate why the Devil wanted the body of Moses—perhaps he wanted his body in a place where people could come and worship him, because the Devil loves to foster dead religions. The Devil was defeated in this endeavor, however, because God would not let the Devil create a mecca to which pilgrims could travel to worship a dead person.

But God superintended over Moses' death, and He "buried him in a valley in the land of Moab, over against Beth-peor: but no man knoweth of his sepulchre unto this day" (Deut. 34:6). God cared for His servant during his lifetime; He also cared for him in his death.

Friend, is the God of Moses your God also? Do you realize how much God cares for you? God does not change; He loves His own even in death. Perhaps you say, "But Moses was a man of special character and total obedience." So he was, but this characteristic is possible for any believer today. The Christian who has obedience to God as his rule of life experiences the joy of knowing the same God that Moses knew.

God had a special relationship with Moses, for He knew him "face to face" (v. 10). So precious was this relationship that God would not even permit the angels to bury Moses. What an example this is of the faithfulness of God to His own! Just as God had been faithful to Moses in his life, so He was faithful to him in his death.

What a great God we have! He is not only faithful to us during our lifetime with the various special needs we have, but He is also faithful to us even in death. Remember that Moses' God is our God; He is a never-changing God.

Notice especially that Moses did not die from some disease in his old age. The Bible says, "Moses was an hundred and twenty years old when he died: his eye was not dim, nor his natural force abated" (v. 7). Moses did not die as a withered, feeble old man but in the fullness of strength. Time had only made him venerable but not weak.

Lessons From Moses' Death

It is greatly interesting to trace Moses' life from the brink of a river, where he lay as a helpless baby, to the top of Pisgah, where he stood in the company of his God and gazed with undimmed vision on the inheritance of Israel. Think of it—120 years between those two events. They were years of serving and believing God for his own needs and for the needs of his people. No other life is so described in the Bible as Moses'.

None of us is called of God to a position in service as Moses had. But every believer is called of God to give the kind of service Moses did—each one is to be faithful. The Bible says, "Moreover it is required in stewards, that a man be found faithful" (I Cor. 4:2). Because as believers in Jesus Christ we are the stewards of God, it is exceedingly important that we be faithful in our service. God says, "Be thou faithful unto death, and I will give thee a crown of life" (Rev. 2:10).

Several important lessons can be gleaned from Moses' death. First, in death we, too, stand alone. We may not be absolutely alone as Moses was—there may be friends and loved ones around us—but in a real sense we are alone with God no matter who else is there. This is why each person needs to be sure of his individual relationship with God.

Second, we meet God on our own record, not on someone else's. As Moses faced God in death, his mother's or his father's relationship with God was not important. Only his own relationship with God mattered. So it is with each one of us; each one is responsible for his own personal relationship with the Lord.

Third, all that surrounded Moses' death was "according to the word of the Lord" (Deut. 34:5). Our lives and deaths are also ordered by God. Concerning man, Job 14:5 says, "Seeing his days are determined, the number of his months are with thee, thou hast appointed his bounds that he cannot pass." No one knows the time of his death, when he will be required to give account to God, but this time has been determined by the Lord.

Fourth, the death of a saint is precious in God's eyes. God exercised loving care over Moses at death, and every believer's death somehow brings glory to the Lord. The psalmist said, "Precious in the sight of the Lord is the death of his saints" (Ps. 116:15). John 21:19 also indicates that a believer's death glorifies the Lord. Jesus had explained how Peter would die, and verse 19 records: "This spake he, signifying by what death he should glorify God."

Fifth, the Lord takes no pleasure in the death of the wicked. Moses had been dearly beloved by God, and he would be in the presence of God immediately after his death. But this is not true of an unbeliever; thus, Ezekiel 33:11 says, "As I live, saith the Lord God, I have no pleasure in the death of the wicked."

Sixth, the Lord knows where all the bodies of the dead are. Just as the Lord knew where Moses' body was even though no one else did, God also knows the location of the remains of every dead person. Although the remains of a body of a believer may have turned to dust long ago, that believer's body will be resurrected from the grave when the Lord Jesus Christ returns. The Bible says, "For the Lord himself shall descend from heaven with a shout, with the voice of the archangel, and with the trump of God: and the dead in Christ shall rise first" (I Thess. 4:16).

The Lord not only knows where the remains of believers are, but He also knows where the remains of unbelievers are. The unsaved dead of all ages will someday be resurrected to stand before the Great White Throne Judgment: "And I saw a great white throne, and him that sat on it, from whose face the earth and the heaven fled away; and there was found no place for them. And I saw the dead, small and great, stand before God; and the books were opened: and another book was opened, which is the book of life: and the dead were judged out of those things which were written in the books, according to their works. And the sea gave up the dead which were in it; and death and hell delivered up the dead which were in them: and they were judged every man according to their works. And death and hell were cast into the lake of fire. This is the second death. And whosoever was not found written in the book of life was cast into the lake of fire" (Rev. 20:11-15).

But remember, God receives no pleasure from the death of the wicked (Ezek. 33:11). What God desires is that each person believe in Jesus Christ as his personal Saviour. John 1:12 assures us, "As many as received him, to them gave he power to become the sons of God, even to them that believe on his name." John 5:24 says, "He that heareth my word, and believeth on him that sent me, hath everlasting life, and shall not come into condemnation; but is passed from death unto life." First John 5:12 promises, "He that hath the Son hath life; and he that hath not the Son of God hath not life." If you do not know Jesus Christ as your Saviour, may you realize your sinful condition and place your trust in Him as your Saviour from condemnation before it is eternally too late.

The Mount of Triumph

It was not the end of the story when Moses saw the Promised Land and died before the Lord and was buried by God. There is a glorious sequel—the overwhelming disappointment of not being able to enter the land had a joyous destiny.

Nebo and Pisgah were not the last mountains on which Moses was destined to stand. About 1500 years after Moses was on Nebo and Pisgah, he appeared on another mountain with Elijah and the Lord Jesus Christ—the Mount of Transfiguration.

The Gospel of Luke records that Jesus "took Peter and John and James, and went up into a mountain to pray. And as he prayed, the fashion of his countenance was altered, and his raiment was white and glistering. And, behold, there talked with him two men, which were Moses and Elias [Elijah]: who appeared in glory, and spake of his decease [departure] which he should accomplish at Jerusalem" (9:28-31).

The desire of Moses' heart had at last been granted! He had yearned to enter the land, but God had not permitted him to do so earlier. However, he appeared in the land not only with Elijah but also with the Lord Jesus Christ Himself. God had given Moses a foretaste of the glory that was to follow by allowing him to view the land from the top of Pisgah. Then he actually entered the Promised Land in the company of the Lord of Glory.

On the Mount of Transfiguration notice that Moses and Elijah "spake of his decease which he should accomplish at Jerusalem" (v. 31). The Transfiguration occurred just prior to the Lord's going to the cross to shed His blood for the sin of the world, and Moses and Elijah were encouraging the Lord concerning what He had to face.

The fact that Moses was not able to enter the land during his lifetime but was able to do so later is a lesson to us that final reward does not always come here and now. The believer's greatest rewards are future. In a sense, this can be spoken of as a "delayed reward." Great men of faith never have to have the reward at the present—they look to a reward that is beyond. This is evident from Hebrews 11, which says of great men of faith, "All these, having gained approval through their faith, did not receive what was promised, because God had provided something better for us, so that apart from us they should not be made perfect" (vv. 39,40, NASB).

The glorious thing to remember is that God has a plan whereby we share in future rewards. Therefore, it is imperative that we keep our eyes on the future and on the glories that will come later. What a joy it will be to someday sit with Abraham, Isaac and Jacob, as well as Moses and Elijah, to rejoice in the God of our salvation!

God's rewards for Moses' faithful service did not come during his lifetime, but they resulted from a decision he made at the age of 40. "By faith Moses, when he was come to years, refused to be called the son of Pharaoh's daughter; choosing rather to suffer affliction with the people of God, than to enjoy the pleasures of sin for a season; esteeming the reproach of Christ greater riches than the treasures in Egypt: for he had respect unto the recompence of the reward" (Heb. 11:24-26). On the Mount of Transfiguration Moses was beginning to see the full and rich rewards for the decision he had made over 1500 years earlier.

This same principle is also true for the believer today. His rewards are primarily future. In fact, the last chapter of the Bible records these words of the Lord Jesus Christ: "Behold, I come quickly; and my reward is with me, to give every man according as his work shall be" (Rev. 22:12).

Stages of Moses' Rewards

Moses' rewards came in different stages. First, he was given an unparalleled view of the Promised Land from the vantage point of Mount Nebo. Second, he stood with Elijah and the Lord on the Mount of Transfiguration. Third, he still has a special reward awaiting him in connection with the Second Coming of the Lord Jesus Christ. This third aspect is a debatable one, but it is my personal conviction that Moses will be one of the two witnesses spoken of in Revelation 11.

During the Tribulation the Antichrist will kill everyone who refuses to worship him. But in the middle of the seven-year Tribulation, God will bring in two witnesses, of whom it is said: "I will give power unto my two witnesses, and they shall prophesy a thousand two hundred and threescore days, clothed in sackcloth" (v. 3). The two witnesses prophesy for three and a half years, which is a reminder to us that God is never without a witness, even during the darkest times of spiritual declension.

Concerning the two witnesses, God said, "If any man will hurt them, fire proceedeth out of their mouth, and devoureth their enemies: and if any man will hurt them, he must in this manner be killed. These have power to shut heaven, that it rain not in the days of their prophecy: and have power over waters to turn them to blood, and to smite the earth with all plagues, as often as they will" (vv. 5,6).

If one of these witnesses is Moses, then the indication is that God will give him a final opportunity to be vindicated before men. While on earth, Moses never vindicated himself; he suffered along with God's people without complaint. But if he is one of the two witnesses, it is clear that God will vindicate him before all mankind.

Although the Bible does not specifically say who the two witnesses are, it is interesting to observe that they will perform miracles similar to those performed by Moses and Elijah. Elijah prevented rain during his ministry (see I Kings 17:1; James 5:17,18), and Moses brought plagues on Pharaoh and the Egyptians (see Ex. 7—12).

If the two witnesses are Moses and Elijah, this is another reward of God for their faithfulness. But notice what will happen to the two witnesses: "When they shall have finished their testimony, the beast that ascendeth out of the bottomless pit shall make war against them, and shall overcome them, and kill them. And their dead bodies shall lie in the street of the great city, which spiritually is called

Sodom and Egypt, where also our Lord was crucified. And they of the people and kindreds and tongues and nations shall see their dead bodies three days and a half, and shall not suffer their dead bodies to be put in graves. And they that dwell upon the earth shall rejoice over them, and make merry, and shall send gifts one to another; because these two prophets tormented them that dwelt on the earth" (Rev. 11:7-10).

But even though God permits the two witnesses to be killed, notice their ultimate triumph: "After three days and an half the spirit of life from God entered into them, and they stood upon their feet; and great fear fell upon them which saw them. And they heard a great voice from heaven saying unto them, Come up hither. And they ascended up to heaven in a cloud; and their enemies beheld them" (vv. 11,12).

As I read this passage and think of Moses, again I ask the question, Could this not be God's final vindication of Moses in the presence of the whole world? Moses died alone, unseen by men, but if one of the two witnesses is Moses, he will be allowed to die in the sight of all men and to be taken to heaven in the sight of all men.

No one knows where Moses' grave was, but during the Tribulation the two witnesses will be seen ascending into heaven. Inasmuch as the Scriptures do not specifically state who the two witnesses are, we must not be dogmatic. But if they are Moses and Elijah—and I personally believe they will be—it would certainly be a fitting reward for these Old Testament prophets.

Conclusion

In bringing to a close the study of the life of Moses, let us remember the progress in Moses' life. He died to self when he went to Pharaoh to deliver the Israelites from Egypt. He died by himself on Mount Nebo after God had permitted him to view the Promised Land. He encouraged Christ concerning His death when he appeared with Elijah on the Mount of Transfiguration. And—if he is one of the two witnesses—he will be vindicated by God before all mankind.

Moses was great in his birth, great in his decisions, great

in his faithfulness and great in his death. Because he lived by faith, his life still speaks to us, even though he is dead.

Among the many lessons we learn from Moses, none could be greater than realizing the need to be in right relationship to God. Do you realize that "all have sinned, and come short of the glory of God"? (Rom. 3:23). Although none of us can escape condemnation by our own efforts (see Eph. 2:8,9), Jesus Christ shed His blood on the cross and thereby became the satisfaction for our sins. "He is the propitiation [satisfaction] for our sins: and not for our's only, but also for the sins of the whole world" (I John 2:2).

But no one is automatically delivered from condemnation just because Jesus Christ died on the cross. It is necessary to receive Him as Saviour by placing one's faith in Him. "As many as received him, to them gave he power to become the sons of God, even to them that believe on his name" (John 1:12). When any person trusts Jesus Christ as his personal Saviour, he is delivered from condemnation and passes from death to life (John 5:24). If you have not placed your trust in Jesus Christ as your Saviour, do so while there is yet time.